KT-594-416

KEY

1	CATO STREET	8	H.A.C. ARTILLERY GROUND
2	BOW STREET	9	SPAFIELDS
3	WHITE STREET	10	GROSVENOR SQUARE
4	FOX COURT	11	CASLON'S TYPE FOUNDRY
5	MANSION HOUSE	12	KING STREET BARRACKS
6	GREYSTOKE PLACE	13	KNIGHTSBRIDGE BARRACKS
7	NEWGATE PRISON	14	ALBANY STREET BARRACKS

To the Tower

REGENCY
REVOLUTION

THE CASE OF
ARTHUR THISTLEWOOD

Endpapers adapted from a map of 1832
(*Greater London Council Map Collection*).

The Spa Fields Gang, 1816:
Doctor Watson, Thistlewood, Preston and Hooper
(*Archives Department, Westminster City Library*)

REGENCY
REVOLUTION

THE CASE OF
ARTHUR THISTLEWOOD

———

DAVID JOHNSON

COMPTON RUSSELL

In affectionate memory of
Winifred Gladys Johnson, Robert Arthur Johnson
and Kathleen Irene Cattanach

© David Johnson 1974

First published in Great Britain 1974
by Compton Russell Ltd.,
Compton Chamberlayne, Salisbury.
Designed by Humphrey Stone and printed
at Compton Chamberlayne by the
Compton Press.

Contents

Illustrations between pp. 78-79

Also by David Johnson

NOVELS

Sabre General
Promenade in Champagne
Lanterns in Gascony
A Candle in Aragon

JACKDAWS

Clive of India
The Monmouth Rebellion and the Bloody Assizes
The Tower of London
Elizabeth Fry and Prison Reform
Marlborough
The Anglo-Boer War
The American Revolution
London's Peelers and the British Police
Clipper Ships and the 'Cutty Sark'
Alfred the Great
The American Civil War
Gordon at Khartoum

ACKNOWLEDGEMENTS

The author wishes to thank the staffs of the Public
Record Office; the Guildhall Library; the British
Museum; the Local History Section, Westminster
City Library, Marylebone Road; and the Local
History Section, Borough of Camden Library,
Theobald's Road.

Thistlewood and his Associates
1816–20

THE SPA FIELDS GANG

Arthur Thistlewood John Keens or Kearns
James Watson, senior James Watson, junior
Thomas Preston John Castle
John Hooper

THE CATO STREET CONSPIRATORS

Arthur Thistlewood William Davidson
John Thomas Brunt Richard Tidd
James Ings

Robert Adams James Gilchrist
John Monument John Harrison
Charles Cooper James Wilson
Richard Bradburn John Shaw Strange

Also arrested in 1820

Thomas Preston Abel Hall
Robert George John Simmons
Thomas Hazard John Palin
John Firth

Members of the Establishment

The Treasury Solicitor was the Regency equivalent of the modern Director of Public Prosecutions. In 1817 the post was held by Henry Charles Litchfield and in 1820 by George Maule.

Alderman Matthew Wood was Lord Mayor of the City of London for 1815/16 and 1816/17 and Member of Parliament for the City from 10 June 1817 until his death in 1843.

In times of great degeneracy and corruption, the magistrate may expect not only to go unpunished, but to be rewarded for transgressing his duty. He may hope to be a gainer by acts of injustice and oppression.

W. FINCH, *Religion! Liberty! and Laws! ! !*
Reflections on the Case of Despard, 1803

Hell is a city much like London. PERCY BYSSHE SHELLEY

1
The Leader from France

ALTHOUGH the defeat of Bonaparte brought peace to Europe, it was followed by much hardship in England. For nearly twenty years the British Government had been fighting a major war, spending vast sums in the process. Now it was all over. Manufacturers who had thrived on war contracts went bankrupt, while thousands of discharged soldiers and seamen came home to look for work. Rates and taxes rose, wages fell and unemployment soared; labourers went road-making for half a crown a week and skilled workmen pawned their tools. By 1816 the economy was on the point of collapse.

For years past the Radical leaders had been blaming England's voting system for the plight of the 'labouring poor'. Now, in the slump which followed Waterloo, the labouring poor began to listen. Radical orators found that more and more people were turning out to hear them preach parliamentary reform – to the alarm and disgust of the squirearchy. 'Their professed object is a reform in Parliament,' wrote a gentleman at Bolton to the Home Office, 'but their real one is believed to be a Revolution in the State.' A number of provincial magistrates asked the Home Secretary to send them pikes and a troop of cavalry. 'The word Revolution is in very common use,' warned Colonel Shaw of Nottingham.

The Home Secretary, Lord Sidmouth, was a very experienced Minister in a very experienced Government. Except for Grenville's brief Ministry of 1806/7, the Tories had been in office since 1784, and England has seldom been governed by men so used to power. Lord Liverpool, Prime Minister since 1812, had been Foreign Secretary, Secretary for War, and Home Secretary twice. Sidmouth was a former Prime Minister. Yet, despite its experience, the Government seemed to be taking undue risks. In 1816 there were barely 16,000 regular troops left in the kingdom, and most of the militia had been stood down. In the provinces maintenance of law and order rested mainly on the mounted Yeomanry, with a strength of perhaps 35,000; in London the Establishment relied on the Foot Guards, a few squadrons of cavalry, and the police magistrates.

Since those days the term 'police magistrate' has lost its original meaning, but in Regency London it was an exact description. A police magistrate had direct control over the policemen attached to his Office. This gave him a dangerous degree of power, especially since he could try and punish petty felons in his own court.

By tradition, the doyen of London's police magistrates was the senior magistrate at Bow Street, the oldest of all the Public Offices, established in Covent Garden since 1739.[1] His official title was Chief Magistrate, and in many ways he was the Regency equivalent of the modern Metropolitan Police Commissioner. On special occasions he took charge of all London's police forces, and was the Home Secretary's chief adviser on law and order in the Metropolis. In 1816 the incumbent was Sir Nathaniel Conant, who had been a police magistrate since 1792, and his Chief Clerk at Bow Street was John Stafford.

Stafford was a most unusual character, who did the work of three ordinary men. In modern terms, he combined the functions of Bow Street's Chief Clerk with those of two senior Scotland Yard officials – Head of the C.I.D., and Assistant Commissioner (Operations). It was Stafford's responsibility to supervise the police phalanx in potentially dangerous situations. He also recruited Home Office spies, transmitted their orders and received their reports. When a spy or an informer was required to make a deposition, Stafford helped him to draft it.

*   *   *

Towards the end of 1816 Conant and Stafford were making plans to police a rally to be held in November at Clerkenwell's Spa Fields. It was a site which the Government particularly mistrusted for public meetings: in just over half an hour a mob could march from Spa Fields to the Bank of England, and in ten minutes more to the Tower. The main speaker was to be the famous Radical orator Henry Hunt; the organisers were members of the obscure Spencean Society.

The Spencean Philanthropists met (chiefly at public houses in London) to talk about land reform and other Radical ideas. Although they were supposed to have formed provincial branches, Francis Place[2] believed that the membership never exceeded fifty. 'The Land is the People's Farm' was a favourite Spencean slogan : they advocated sharing out all the land in the kingdom equally, reckoning that there was enough to give every man, woman and child seven acres each.

The Society's best known members were James Watson and his aggressive young son, also named James, who was usually referred to as Young Watson or Jem. Watson *père* was a fifty-year-old apothecary who styled himself 'Doctor and Surgeon'. Lincolnshire-born, he had practised in many places, including Cheadle in Staffordshire, where (according to an acquaintance) he had been quite prosperous. Later he fell on hard times : when one of his ten children, a girl, died in infancy, Watson claimed that the bed on which she lay dying had been taken away because he could not pay his rent.

It was 'Doctor' Watson who recruited the Society's standard-bearer, a strapping Yorkshireman named John Castle, then aged about thirty. A whitesmith by trade, Castle was living on his wits that autumn [1816], and had been doing so for some time. When Watson first asked him to join the Society, Castle was reluctant, pointing out that he only had 'his little business' to live on. Watson assured him that the Spenceans 'would find him something better to do' and that they had 'plenty of money for everything'. That was good enough for Castle. He joined the Society and became one of the Doctor's inner circle. Apart from Young Watson, there were two others : a drink-sodden buffoon named Thomas Preston, who earned his living as a shoemaker, and Arthur Thistlewood.

Thistlewood was illegitimate. At the time of his birth, his mother had been living with a well-to-do Lincolnshire farmer, who gave the child his surname and paid for him to have a decent education. As a young man Arthur Thistlewood visited Revolutionary Paris, returning to England about 1794. Four years later he was gazetted ensign in the First West Yorks Militia.* When the supplementary militia was raised he obtained his lieutenancy in the Third Lincolnshire and went out to the West Indies, where his brother officers thought him 'a good drill' but much too fond of gambling and women. Soon after reaching the Indies he gave up his commission in rather mysterious circumstances; in later life it was not a subject he cared to discuss.

All kinds of lurid and implausible stories were told about the next phase of his career. It was said that he visited America, went again to France, joined the French Army and served as a grenadier officer under Masséna, notably at the victory of Zurich. There was also a rumour, which eventually found its way into *The Times*, that he had been involved in 'Despard's Business', a plot to kill the King and overthrow the Government in 1802. Thistlewood himself never denied these stories (they undoubtedly helped his Radical image) and used to boast that he had been in five or six revolutions. Probably his past was less colourful than the rumours painted it, but in one respect at least his reputation was justified : he was an expert swordsman.

Back in England in 1804, he married a Lincolnshire lady of fortune with an income of £300 a year; but she died within two years, and it fell out that she had only a life interest in the fortune, which reverted to her family. Thistlewood's in-laws paid him a small allowance until he got into trouble over unpaid debts. When an uncle died, leaving him a farm said to be worth £10,000, he exchanged it for an annuity, but this lapsed two years later when the guarantor went bankrupt.

His second marriage was to Susan Wilkinson, a Horncastle butcher's daughter, a 'genteel little woman' who approved of Thistlewood's Republican principles and accepted his illegitimate son, Julian.† With her dowry Thistlewood bought a farm near

---

* *London Gazette,* 14-28 August 1798.

† It was rumoured that when Thistlewood was courting his first wife he seduced one of her family's servants, and that Julian was the result.

Horncastle, and when that failed he moved to London. In 1816 he was forty-two years old, an embittered adventurer who, it seemed, would never amount to much. There is no doubt that he was a violent and dangerous man. A friend of his who ran a lunatic asylum at Plaistow, and was thus a good judge of such matters, said of him that he was 'fit only for a strait waistcoat'.

In 1816, most surprisingly, John Stafford and the police spies of Bow Street had never heard of him.

* * *

Castle duly carried the banner at the Spa Fields rally, which was held on 15 November. A strong body of police commanded by John Stafford kept a watching brief and mingled with the crowd, which behaved peacefully enough. A petition which called for universal male suffrage and other Radical measures was approved, and Hunt tried to deliver it to the Prince Regent, but in vain. A second rally was arranged for 2 December.

By late November some alarming predictions about this second rally were reaching the Home Office. From the Fleet Prison a man who claimed to have held captain's rank wrote: 'The general object is Burn and destroy all the Jails in the Metropolis, and let out the prisoners.' Even more disturbing was a letter written by a Suffolk clergyman to Twining's, the tea and coffee merchants in the Strand, warning them of a large body of workmen which was moving towards London. 'On Friday night last not less than thirty slept in this parish on their way – and in that ratio for a fortnight past.' An anonymous note to the Home Office declared: 'The meeting in Spa Fields is aware of the Collection of Soldiers in this vicinity. The appearance of Troops will occasion the destruction of London. Twenty thousand Englishmen can set any city in such flames as no Engines can extinguish.'

When 2 December dawned, the Home Office was expecting an attack on the Tower and the Artillery Ground at Bunhill Row, Finsbury, headquarters of the Honourable Artillery Company, where four cannon and 250 stand of small arms were kept. Lord Sidmouth had passed on much of the Home Office's information to the Lord Mayor, Matthew Wood. Placing men at intervals between the City and Spa Fields, with orders to send him reports of the rally every half-hour, Wood took post himself at the Mansion House.

The police magistrates had instructions to report the state of their districts to the Home Office every two hours, while in the City and the Borough of Southwark troops were standing to arms. A squadron of Dragoons was in the Light Horse Volunteers' H.Q. in Gray's Inn Lane,* and a detachment of Life Guards had been sent to Kesterton's Stables near London Bridge. There was a double guard at the Horse Guards, the Tower and the British Museum, and a Serjeant's Guard at the King's Bench Prison. Every prison warden knew where the nearest soldiers could be found.

The crowds which made their way to Clerkenwell included hundreds of people who, having first been to Newgate to watch four men hanged, went on to Spa Fields afterwards. Once again John Stafford was at the Fields with a strong force of police, including about eighty men from Bow Street's total of just over a hundred.

Hunt arrived late at Spa Fields that day, probably on purpose. At the rally in November he had addressed the crowd from the window of a small public house called Merlin's Cave, which had been the focal point of the meeting. But on 2 December, according to John Stafford, there was a lot of activity round a four-wheeled waggon stationed near the chapel, towards Coppice Row. The men in this waggon, from which the horses had been removed, had two flags and a calico banner. The latter was inscribed 'The Brave Soldiers are our Brothers. Treat them kindly.' Jem Watson, one of the group, made an inflammatory speech; then, jumping to the ground, he began to make his way out of the Fields, followed by the flag-bearers and some of the crowd.

John Stafford went into action. Wresting the pole of one flag from its bearer he tried to break it, then, finding it too sturdy, forced it to the ground and stood on it. A Hatton Garden police

* Now Gray's Inn Road.

officer tackled the man with the banner and jumped on the staff until it snapped. Young Watson and his followers streamed away to Smithfield and the City.

The first prison in their line of march was Newgate. When the Keeper heard that a mob was approaching he sent a messenger to get help from Alderman Wood, but the Lord Mayor could not be found. An urgent call for help was then made to the cavalry at Gray's Inn Lane, who explained regretfully that they could only act on orders from a magistrate. 'If we are not immediately assisted,' wrote the Keeper at a quarter to two, 'we shall be lost.'

At the Royal Exchange the mob encountered the Lord Mayor with a small force of police. The pole of the surviving flag got jammed in one of the iron gratings over the Exchange cellar, and it was captured by Sir James Shaw, the City's Member of Parliament. Several men were arrested here, including a sailor named John Cashman,* who was later described as being 'very drunk', and a labourer named John Hooper. Hooper, who was treasurer to the Spa Fields Organising Committee, was armed with two loaded pistols.

Part of the mob straggled away through the Minories to Tower Hill. Here a man hoisted himself up on to a railing and shouted at the Guardsmen who were standing on the Tower ramparts; seemingly, he was trying to make them open the gates and join the crowd. According to a stockjobber named Heywood, he waved a cutlass as he shouted at the soldiers, offering them double pay and saying that he would make privates into captains. 'There was an Alarm of the Horse coming,' said Heywood, 'upon which the Man got down from the rails, put his Cutlass under his coat, and walked quietly away as if nothing had happened.'

On the way from Spa Fields the rioters had broken into a number of gunsmiths' shops and carried off large numbers of firearms, which they loaded to the muzzle with anything from bullets to knee buckles. In the Minories one shop alone lost seventy or more fowling-pieces and eighty brace of pistols, plus

---

* Cashman was subsequently hanged for his part in the riot.

about thirty swords, twenty pikes, some dirks and a three-pounder carronade. Soon after the incident on Tower Hill, however, the mob began to disperse, leaving the City authorities to clear up the mess.

From the Minories, Castle went back to Tower Hill. Seeing soldiers out on the streets, he decided that it was time to make himself scarce. Walking up Mark Lane he entered a small public house and stayed there until it was almost dark, highly conscious of the fact that he had a pair of stolen pistols in his bosom. After leaving the public house he went to an address near Fetter Lane, where he found Preston, both the Watsons, and Thistlewood. According to Castle, Thistlewood commented that the people were 'not ripe enough to act', and said that he and the Watsons were going into the country. Castle asked him if Young Watson had shot anybody, and Thistlewood replied that he did not know.

At eleven o'clock that night, as the two Watsons and Thistlewood were walking through Highgate, they were mistaken for footpads by Charles Miell of the Bow Street Horse Patrol. Thistlewood and Jem Watson both fired pistols at Miell and managed to escape, but the Doctor was arrested and locked up for the night in the watchhouse at Somers Town. He would not tell Miell his name, but boasted that it would be well known at Bow Street Public Office.

Next day he was questioned at Bow Street by John Stafford, who knew him as a leading Spencean. Although Watson refused to identify the two men who had tried to shoot Miell at Highgate, Stafford was sure that one of them must be the Doctor's son, who was now the most wanted man in London. During the riot a man named Platt had tried to restrain Young Watson from looting a gunshop near the Old Bailey. Young Watson had shot him in the stomach.

*   *   *

The handbills advertising the Spa Fields rally (signed 'John Dyall, chairman – Thomas Preston, secretary') had asked for subscriptions to be sent to 9 Greystoke Place, Fetter Lane. Shortly after midnight of 2 December, the Lord Mayor led a party of police to that address, which turned out to be a poorly furnished house in an alley. There they found Thomas Preston, the drunken secretary of the Organising Committee.

On 7 December, having examined all the prisoners arrested in the City during the riot, the Lord Mayor informed the Home Secretary that he believed Preston, Hooper and the elder Watson were the ringleaders. John Stafford was not convinced. In the first place, several eye-witnesses had mentioned another man who seemed very active in the riot. This man had not been arrested, in Stafford's opinion, nor even properly described. And who was the armed man who had escaped with Jem Watson at Highgate?

The more Stafford probed, the more the identity of this shadowy figure intrigued and challenged him. On 5 December Stafford had questioned John Dyall, the Chairman of the Spa Fields Committee, whose name had appeared with Preston's on the handbills. Dyall described a visit which he made in November to 9 Greystoke Place, where Doctor Watson was lodging at the time. Preston and both the Watsons had been there, together with a man whom Doctor Watson had said was either a military or a naval officer – Dyall could not quite remember which.

What Dyall *did* remember was that this man was thin and about five foot eight inches tall. He wore a blue coat, brown greatcoat and boots, looked like an officer and a gentleman, and seemed to Dyall to be a person of authority. He had sent out for some refreshments and given Dyall two shillings out of his own pocket. Though Dyall was clearly a figurehead and nonentity, his story was none the less interesting for that.

Two days later Stafford examined the landlord of the Carlisle tavern in Shoreditch, one of the places where Spencean meetings were held. The landlord recalled that in November his parlour had been hired for a meeting which thirty or forty men attended. The bill came to six shillings and sixpence, which was paid by a man who tendered a Bank of England ten pound note; but as the landlord would not change it until it was signed, the man wrote on the back of it 'Thistleway, Southampton Buildings'.

Further information was supplied by the sitting magistrate at Shadwell, who had it from a local tax collector that early in November, before the Spa Fields meeting, a lame shoemaker named Thomas Preston had taken three other men to a public house in Shadwell called the George. There they indulged in some very wild and seditious talk, lamenting the state of the poor and boasting that they could raise a thousand armed men. Preston looked dirty and shabby, but his three friends looked decent and respectable. It appeared from their conversation that one of them was a medical man and another had lately come from France.

Following his arrest and examination, Doctor Watson had been lodged in the Coldbath Fields House of Correction at Clerkenwell. In the second week of December Stafford sent Vincent Dowling there to eavesdrop on Watson's conversations with his visitors.

Dowling was a professional shorthand writer who worked intermittently as a police spy. After a week at Coldbath Fields he submitted three reports, which Stafford passed on to Henry Litchfield, the Treasury Solicitor. According to Dowling, Watson told one visitor that when he left London on the second he had intended going to America; all the leaders of the riot had agreed to do this in the event of failure. 'My son's rashness spoiled all,' he added. 'If he had waited we should have had a greater force to accompany us to the City.'

He talked a good deal about his son :

There were six leaders on the second of December. Myself, my son and Thysselton were three. There were three others. We all left Town on Monday night. There was one with us who had plenty of money. He promised my son and I to take us all to America if our scheme failed . . . If I thought my son was safe I could disclose a good deal . . . I do not like to tell who the other leaders were.

In his third report Dowling wrote : 'The prisoner is preparing his defence, which he is enriching by divers quotations from scripture. He says he is of sound mind.'

The inference is that the spy regarded the Doctor as a crackpot. Nonetheless, if Stafford was looking for proof that there was much more to the Spa Fields affair than met the eye, Dowling's reports supplied it. '*If he had waited, we should have had a greater force. . .*'

The Doctor had at least three bolt-holes in the labyrinth of courts and alleys which spread east from Chancery Lane. In add-ition to the room at 9 Greystoke Place he had lodgings at 1 Dean Street and a surgery in Three Kings Court. He also rented a room in Bloomsbury, at a house in Hyde Street.* All these places were searched by Bow Street officers on Stafford's orders, and at Hyde Street John Vickery found a list of twelve names. None of them bore any resemblance to Thysselton or Thistleway.

As the Chief Clerk sifted the facts in his room at Bow Street Public Office, he saw a pattern beginning to emerge. For a man who fourteen years before had smashed a Jacobin conspiracy in London, it was disturbingly familiar.

The Spa Fields meeting, organised by men who wanted to confiscate land and give it to the poor, had ended in a riot and the theft of hundreds of weapons – well over 400 firearms from two gunshops alone. Tricolour cockades had been worn at Spa Fields and in the streets, prompting a dramatic reference in *The Times* to 'the badge of Corsican France'.

There had been secret meetings at the house in Greystoke Place. The locals said that on certain nights they had noticed men going in quickly and furtively, as if afraid to be seen, while a lookout hung about at the corner of Fetter Lane. If a police-man or strangers approached, the lookout would whistle a parti-cular tune, obviously as a warning signal to the men inside the house.

There was, too, a very interesting detail in the Shadwell magi-strate's report, which many men might have overlooked, but which to Stafford would have stood out like a wrong date in a deposition : one of the men who talked sedition at the George in Shadwell 'had lately come from France'. As Stafford knew, the restoration of the Bourbons had forced all kinds of Republican *canaille* to emigrate from France, including some expatriate Eng-

* Now West Central Street. The room was actually a small shop, but Watson's son often slept in it.

lishmen and many Irish. It seemed quite possible, therefore, that the leadership of the Spencean Society had been taken over by a British Jacobin.

One thing was clear. Whatever the evil might be that was hatching in the rookeries of Holborn and the City, the key to it had been at 9 Greystoke Place.

*   *   *

By mid-December the papers were giving it out that one of the men who had escaped at Highgate was Thisselton, an active member of the 'Spa Fields Gang', who had lately returned from the Continent. Since the name Thisselton could only have come from Bow Street, it must be assumed that Stafford had leaked it to the Press. If so, it quickly had the desired result. The Home Office received a letter, signed 'J.H.' and bearing no address, marked for the attention of Lord Sidmouth. It informed his lordship that the man whom the papers kept referring to as Thisselton was very probably Arthur Thistlewood of Horncastle, a man of bad principles who hated the Government.

2

Stafford Recruits a Spy

EACH Public Office was responsible for its own territory but, because of its seniority and experience, Bow Street had a much wider brief. The Chief Magistrate's office operated the capital's Horse and Foot Patrols, and even sent Runners to investigate crimes outside London.

A force of eight or nine Runners, who were plain-clothes police officers, was attached to every Public Office except Wapping. Like all other London policemen, a Runner who did a particularly good job, such as recovering valuable stolen goods, was allowed to accept a reward. This system led to serious abuses : in 1816 a man was actually bribed to organise a robbery by a Bow Street Patrole,* who intended to 'solve' the crime and collect the reward. Significantly, the slang name for the Runners in Regency London was 'The Traps'. The ones at Bow Street were the best known. They were also the most successful, partly because Bow Street could afford to pay a high price for information.

Runners got their information in different ways. Sometimes, if his spy or 'nose' failed to find out what he wanted to know, the Trap would put on a simple disguise, assume a false name, and become a spy himself. Thus early in 1817, under an alias, George Ruthven was regularly attending meetings of the Spencean Philanthropists. Though only twenty-four, Ruthven had nearly eight years' police experience to his credit and courage to burn : he frequently took the most hair-raising risks, and seemed to enjoy doing so.

He found that the Spenceans spent most of their meetings

---

* 'Patrole' was the name given to members of the Horse and Foot Patrols.

debating nonsensical questions* and drinking cheap wine. When a debate ended the meeting 'proceeded to harmony', which meant that a member was called upon to stand up and sing. Not all members complied; after the 9 January meeting Ruthven reported, 'Mr. Cannon (who cannot sing) voluntarily gave an obscene paraphrase of the first Psalm.' The following week, at the Nag's Head in Carnaby Market, the proceedings dissolved into uproar at the Secretary's announcement that he had decided to abolish 'smoaking'.

The Prince Regent was a favourite butt of the Spenceans, who liked to sing a song which began 'There lives a hog in Pall Mall' to the tune of 'Sweet Lass of Richmond Hill'. At one meeting, when the Secretary read out a newspaper account of the people cheering the Prince, a member announced that it was a lie: nobody had cheered the Regent, he insisted, except a guinea pig in a tree.

As part of each report, Ruthven named all the members who attended the meetings, but whether these were held at the Cock in Soho, the Mulberry Tree in Moorfields, the Carlisle in Shoreditch or the Pineapple in Lambeth, the names never varied much. It was obvious that the Spencean Society was a very small one – the joining fee of a shilling was no doubt partly to blame. It was true that Spenceans often addressed a wider audience in public houses when there was no room available for a private meeting, but their speeches usually aroused good-natured derision.

In spite of all the buffoonery, by the end of January Ruthven was beginning to think that he might not be wasting his time after all. Attendances had increased to fifty, then to eighty or more, and on 30 January at least 130 met at the Mulberry Tree. 'I suspect there is something more serious at the Bottom than I am aware of at the moment,' he wrote. 'But I think I shall find it out.'

Meanwhile, an official in Manchester had written to warn

---

* e.g. 'Is the American Government to be applauded or condemned for the means they have adopted to civilise the Indians by giving them a portion of their land?'

Lord Sidmouth of 'a general union of the lower orders through-
out the country', and in London there were stories of messages
such as 'Give us Bread, Or the Regent's Head!' being pinned
to blood-smeared loaves and left at the gates of Carlton House.
At the end of the month the Regent's coach was stoned as he
drove to open Parliament.

*   *   *

Surprisingly, there was no reward out yet for Thistlewood.
Young Watson, on the other hand, had 'weighed' £500 since
6 December. He was first hidden by an engraver in Bayham
Street, Camden Town, but the presence of a wanted man so
upset the engraver's wife, who was pregnant, that Watson moved
to a house in Newgate Street. Here the owner provided him
with woman's clothing, in which he used to go for an evening
stroll. He must have been a grotesque sight : the police described
him as having smallpox scars on his face, the left eyelid 'rather
drooping' over the eye, and 'very black teeth'. His face was
further disfigured by vain attempts to remove a mole with
caustic.

From hiding, he wrote to the Lord Mayor claiming that it
was not he who had shot Mr. Platt in the gunshop, though he
knew the man who had. He offered to give himself up, and name
Mr. Platt's assailant, in exchange for the £500 reward which
was out for his arrest and a free pardon.

The Home Office, too, received a number of letters from
people anxious to claim the reward. One of them, a correspon-
dent signing himself 'J.F.', informed Lord Sidmouth that Watson
was staying with Mr. Davey the shoemaker at 2 Church Street,
Lambeth. As soon as his arrest was announced, J.F. proposed
to call at Lord Sidmouth's office, where he would identify himself by producing a copy of his letter, and claim the £500
reward. 'Them Daveys are sly artful people,' he added. 'The
husband has already been a prisoner in Horsemonger Lane, and
Mrs. D. practises shop-lifting very much.'

*   *   *

A third Spa Fields meeting had been arranged for 10 February.
According to the rumours reaching John Stafford the organisers

planned to turn it into another riot, using the arms which had been captured in December. It would have been an easy matter to have Watson and his under-strappers arrested again, but on the evidence available Stafford believed that it would have been a waste of time. He had already said as much in a letter to the Home Office.

In this interesting document, Stafford had pointed out that those societies which could be suppressed as unlawful combinations and confederacies had been described with great precision by the Statute 39 George III, chapter 79. As he read it, merely to prove that two or three meetings had been held 'for the ostensible purpose of promoting reform', even though inflammatory speeches had been made at them, was not enough. To obtain a conviction under the Act it was essential to introduce a spy into the Society, someone who could gain a complete knowledge of its secrets and become a witness against it.

> This together with their papers and books, if they have any, would form a body of legal testimony upon which the parties might be convicted, either in a summary way before a Magistrate or by indictment, but without evidence such as this and every likelihood of obtaining convictions, it strikes me that prosecutions had better be spared.

This was the position when, either at the end of January or the beginning of February [1817], Jack Castle went down to Bow Street Public Office.

The man whom Watson had chosen as flag-bearer for his height and strength was getting desperate, for the Spenceans were not so well off as the Doctor had boasted, and in Castle's own words he was 'in very great distress'. A few days before his visit to Bow Street, he had been drinking at the Cock in Grafton Street, Soho,* when a man whom he had never seen before asked him to join a plot to kill the Prince Regent. The idea was to ambush the Regent's coach on the Brighton road, thirty or forty miles from London, and shoot him dead.

* Not the modern Grafton Street in Mayfair.

By this stroke of luck, Castle was in a position to earn the Regent's gratitude and a handsome reward; his only fear was that if he approached the police he might be caught out by the conspirators and killed. Hastening down to Broad Street, St. Giles's, he sought out a Bow Street officer of his acquaintance named Salmon and asked his advice.

Salmon assured him that if he went to Bow Street he would be well looked after and that no one would ever know that he had given information. Castle went with him to the Office and met John Stafford. Next morning, said Castle later, 'Mr. Stafford introduced me to Mr. Beckett the Under-Secretary,* who did assure me my safety on condition that I told them the truth, which was a great ease to my mind, and from that moment I entered into Confidential Communication with Mr. Stafford.'

Initially Castle did not tell Stafford the whole truth of his position, though he admitted that he had not worked regularly for some years, and that he had been in trouble four years earlier under the name of Jackson. Stafford knew that the Cock in Grafton Street had been for a long time the Spencean Society's favourite meeting place, and putting two and two together he asked Castle if he had ever been to 9 Greystoke Place. Whether through fear of Thistlewood or some other motive, Castle did not want to admit that such a person even existed, let alone that he had been one of his associates. Trying to bluff it out, he said that although he had been to a house known as Number 9 somewhere near Fetter Lane, he could not swear to its exact address. 'It *might* be Greystoke Place,' he allowed. 'I saw the two Watsons and Preston and another person whose Name I don't recollect, there was a Man whose Name was Thiselton or something like that.'

Stafford realised that he was dealing with a scoundrel, but one whose evidence could be invaluable. On 6 February he summoned Castle to Bow Street and asked him if he had anything more to communicate, and when Castle said that he had not, Stafford put the screw on him.

* John Beckett, Permanent Under-Secretary at the Home Office 1806-17.

I told him he did not deal candidly with me, and that I knew he had not disclosed all that he knew. He declared he had . . . nobody could say anything against him, for he detested violence and bloodshed . . . between violence and getting too much drink many things were talked of that had better not been mentioned, that everything seemed to be known, that he knew he was liable to be brought to Bow Street and publicly examined, that he with others had suffered a great deal from distress and that he did not much care for his life, a Man could only die once.

Stafford's tactics did the trick. The following day Castle reported :

I expect to be measured for Cloathes to-morrow and I must go to the Meeting and I expect Arms will be put into my hands. I shall get away if I can but if I should be taken I expect to be protected. I know I run great risk of Assassination but I am determined to go through with it and report everything . . . I am to meet Watson and Preston to-morrow at one . . . I have had my Whiskers shaved close and I am sure they watch me a great deal . . . I am obliged to prevent Suspicion to say many things that I know to be wrong.

Lord Sidmouth ordered the Chief Magistrate to have the organisers of the Spa Fields meeting arrested next day, 8 February, and Stafford made arrangements for three police raids to go in at precisely the same time. They were postponed at the eleventh hour when Doctor Watson dropped briefly out of sight.

Stafford and two King's Messengers led the three raids, which began just before eight o'clock on Sunday morning, 9 February. Watson and Preston were found in bed together, covered only by a ragged quilt, at a house in King's Head Court, and seemed very reluctant to get up. Also arrested that morning were Castle, a tailor named Keens, Evans (the Spencean Society secretary) and Evans's father. Their papers having been seized and sealed up, they were all taken to Bow Street and given breakfast.

Later that day Castle was questioned by Lord Sidmouth about the projected Spa Fields meeting, and his replies were taken down in shorthand.

Q. Is there anything connected with to-morrow's proceedings which you have to communicate?

A. There is a parcel of people over the water,* there are a quantity of things called *Cats*† made, I believe there are colours to be produced to-morrow. Mr. Preston has got a tri-coloured dress which he means to exhibit himself in tomorrow . . .

Q. Do you know where Thistlewood is?

A. I have no doubt but he is with his wife's friends in Lincolnshire.

Q. Do you know where young Watson is?

A. I think he is likewise in Lincolnshire. I am confident he is not gone out of the country.

A warrant for Arthur Thistlewood was issued next morning. Castle now had nothing to lose by talking, and everything to gain, and to John Stafford he poured out a strange and almost incredible tale. According to Castle, the lists of names found on Doctor Watson and in his lodgings were those of the men who would form the Committee of Public Safety, once the Revolution which Arthur Thistlewood was planning had begun.

*   *   *

It was not the only strange tale told at Bow Street Public Office that month. On 14 February, five days after the arrests, the officer who had taken Castle to meet Stafford was asked what he knew about the man. Salmon stated that in March of 1813 he had been introduced to him by his fellow Patrole Samuel Dickens. Castle and Dickens were both party to a plot, devised by a Transport Board clerk named Sugden, to swindle the rela-

---

* i.e. on the south bank of the Thames.

† Cart-wheels fitted with scythe blades, to be used to cripple cavalry horses.

tives of a rich French prisoner-of-war. The plan was to persuade
the relatives to send money and a boat to help the prisoner to
get back to France. Castle would aid the man's escape and
Dickens would recapture him, ideally with the help of Salmon,
who was invited to join the plot. According to Salmon :

> Castle told me that he had seen Warner and got an order
> from him in Bonaparte's own hand-writing to give £1600
> for bringing over to France Colonel Prevotti or some such
> name, a prisoner of war at Abergavenny . . . The Vessel
> sent from France to pick the Colonel up would be seized,
> as would the money.

Sugden later told Salmon that Castle had bungled the affair
and got himself into gaol.

On the very same day that Salmon made this statement at Bow
Street, Castle was admitted as a witness for the Crown.

3

Prisoners of the State

HELPED by John Stafford, Castle produced a three-part account
of all that had happened between his joining the Spencean
Society and the Spa Fields riot. An approver, as an accomplice
who turned king's evidence was called, needed all the protection
the Crown could give him (especially when two of the men he
was betraying were still at liberty). This is why Castle's statements
bear no signature, and his name never appears in them. They
are headed simply 'Narrative', 'Further Narrative', and 'Conclu-
sion of Narrative'. On the back of them are pencilled the words
'Thistlewood Papers'.

Castle claimed that a month after his first meeting with Doctor
Watson, he had been elected to the Spencean Committee, which
usually met either at 9 Greystoke Place or at Preston's house in
Clement's Inn Passage. He gave some interesting examples of its
transactions:

DOCTOR WATSON: I have made a wonderful discovery
to-day, for I have heard of a place where there is three
or four hundred thousand greatcoats packed up safe,
ready to send abroad, and we will give them to the poor
to keep them warm this winter, and if we once get them
on our side we need not to fear all the land-holders.

THISTLEWOOD: Where are those cloathes?

WATSON: I have been with a Man that has told me how
they are packed up in large packs so that the salt water
cannot get to them nor hurt if they was thrown over-
board: they lay in Somerset House.

MR. THISTLEWOOD AND YOUNG WATSON: That shall be our
head quarters while we get things settled.

Doctor Watson was to be one of the generals of the Revolution, but he had proposed that Thistlewood should be the Head General, 'as he, Thistlewood, found them the whole of the money'. This included the beer money, with which the Head General and Castle treated soldiers in the taverns round Bow Street and Drury Lane. Thistlewood would ask them how much they were paid, and what they thought about their officers.

Castle made regular visits to certain barracks, especially those at King Street and Knightsbridge, 'to see which was the best place for setting them on fire'. The idea was that, when the Revolution began, the garrisons of these burning barracks would be too busy fighting the flames or too affected by the smoke to fight. Thistlewood believed that they would join him once he was in control of the city.

Several pieces of cannon would be seized, some from the Honourable Artillery Company's Headquarters at Bunhill Row, Finsbury, others from the City Light Horse Volunteer Drill Hall in Gray's Inn Lane. As for manpower, some of the labourers who were cutting the Paddington Canal had told Thistlewood that he could count on five or six hundred of them, 'as they wished a good row, and would rather be killed as they had nothing to do'. The porters and coal heavers at the Adelphi wharves, said Castle, had also been approached. Thistlewood expected thousands of London's artisans and labourers to support him, and Preston said he was sure that, being so well known, he himself could raise 15,000 men in half an hour. Since Thistlewood calculated that there were something like 40,000 workers awaiting the signal to rise in London, he would out-number the regular troops and police of the capital by over twenty to one.

The main problem was how to get weapons: the plotters had no money. On one occasion, when Castle said that he knew where he could buy some sabres and pistols cheap, Thistlewood managed to scrape up £3. Castle then bought 'two pair of Pistols at a Pawnbroker's in Paddington and two Sabres at an old Iron Shop in Marylebone'.

To offset the shortage of weapons, when the rising began

'some men were to get on the tops of houses, and if the soldiers
would not join us they were to be destroyed, as a Stone, a Brick,
a Tile or a Bottle thrown from a house would knock a man on
horse down'. The Government's cavalry would be hampered by
barricades and crippled by iron cats. A Navy would be fitted
out 'in the course of a few hours' to stop Wellington's regiments
coming over from France, and a fast sailing vessel would fetch
Bonaparte to London from Saint Helena : 'young Watson was to
go for him.'

In the meantime Young Watson was canvassing soldiers of the
London garrisons, and at the same time making them feel in-
secure and angry with the Government. Castle once heard him
tell a Life Guards trooper that, as the Government did not trust
the Household Cavalry to act loyally in a disturbance, it had
just imported 50,000 soldiers from Russia. The man replied to
the effect that, if the Government actually wanted to cause a
disturbance, it was going the right way about it; but in any
case the Life Guards 'would soon do for the Russians, and would
not be domineered by any foreign troops'. Watson asked him
how he would act if his regiment was called out against the mob,
to which the trooper answered, 'That depends a great deal what
the mob was doing of.'

On the day of the rising, Castle was to offer soldiers who
agreed to join the mob 100 guineas down or double pay for life :
'that sum was calculated up and I think they said it would
amount to two million of Money, but that was nothing to the
National Debt.' The Foot Guards were ripe for defection, in
Thistlewood's opinion, and from his talks with Guardsmen at
the Tower, Castle got the impression that three out of five would
join the mob once the Revolution began.

I said, 'If the Horse Guards were to come down against
you, what chance would you have with them?' They said,
'Damn their eyes, we would soon settle them, for one
Regiment of Foot would beat all the Horse Guards in
London if they come into the streets.' I said, 'How would

you manage that, for I have been in the Surrey Yeomanry
Cavalry and I think two such Regiments as that would beat
yours, if once your ranks were broken.' They said they
would take care and prevent that, for their first two ranks
would kneel down and make a *Chevaux de Frise,** and cut
the Cavalry off from one end of the street to the other.

Castle admitted that he had been at the first Spa Fields
meeting, when he had acted as a flag-bearer, but not at the
December one. Early on 2 December, he claimed, he had drunk
a glass of wine with Thistlewood at the Black Dog in Drury
Lane, then gone to Chancery Lane to put the flags into the
hired waggon. When that was done he had made his way to
London Bridge, where he was supposed to meet a contingent of
smiths, but they never arrived.

His next call had been at Tower Hill, where nothing seemed to
be happening, so he set off to walk to Spa Fields. In Little
Britain, near Smithfield, he encountered the mob. Leading it
were Thistlewood and 'Old Watson', who cried 'To the Tower,
Jack!'

When Jack asked where the others were, Watson told him,
'They will be there before us! Run!'

While Castle was giving all this information to the Home
Secretary, several well-meaning citizens were writing to warn
the Treasury Solicitor that he was a rogue. A spring-blind maker
in Long Acre named William Bayliss said that Castle had had
a quantity of pikeheads made by Isaac Bentley, a smith in Hart
Street, Covent Garden.† According to Bayliss, Castle had ordered
500 of them, but only 250 had been delivered, and these were
too late to be of use. Castle boasted that he had tied them up
in two old nail bags and thrown them into the Thames from
Westminster Bridge, roughly opposite the third arch.

Bayliss had actually seen these pikeheads being made at the

---

* In the sixteenth century the Frisians used portable rows of spikes against
enemy cavalry. The name 'Frisian Horses' was later applied to any similar
sort of defence, and in this case means a row of muskets with fixed bayonets.
† Now Floral Street.

Hart Street forge. Bentley told him that they were going to be used on a park paling in the country, to which Bayliss replied that it must be an uncommonly strong paling if it needed such huge pikes. 'I think when drawn out they were eight or nine inches in length,' he wrote, 'sharp at both ends, but one end jagged to hold fast in the wood.' He believed that Castle had paid Bentley for them, and concluded, 'Castles is a bad man to his King and Country and a thief besides. He stole a sheet off the bed where he lodged and pawned it not long before he was taken up.'

* * *

On 18 February the offer of a £500 reward for Young Watson was renewed, and for the first time a similar amount was offered for Thistlewood. Also that day the report of a Secret Committee of the House of Lords was presented to Parliament.* This Committee had been investigating rumours that a Revolution was being planned, and that a rising in London would be the signal for it to begin. It reported that prisoners in the London gaols were being told that they would soon be freed, and armed by a 'Provisional Government'; in the meantime they were being urged to provide themselves with tricolour cockades. Soldiers of the London garrisons were being sounded out by the plotters, who were planning to manufacture pikes[3] and attack the Tower. The ringleaders, members of Hampden or Spencean clubs, met chiefly in low public houses.

Pikes and tricolour cockades . . . Nothing recalled Jacobin brutality quite so evocatively. These were the weapons on which the heads had been carried during the Terror, and these the emblems – white for France, red and blue for Paris – which had been tied in their hair.

The Report, which plainly owed a good deal to Castle's revelations and the warning letters received at the Home Office the previous year, caused tremendous alarm. The great landowners felt that their estates and possibly their lives were in danger; and because of the system which men like Hunt wanted

---

* *Report of the Secret Committee of the House of Lords,* 1817 [*Reports, Committees,* 1817, *iv*].

to reform, the great landowners of England controlled not only the local government, but Parliament as well.* In their eyes, the Government's first duty was to maintain internal order, and if that meant arresting men and sending them to gaol solely on a warrant from the Home Secretary, so be it. On 28 February the Suspension of the Habeas Corpus Act was carried in the House of Commons.

Meanwhile, the 'approver' Castle was doing his best to please from the prison at Tothill Fields. In a letter addressed to 'Mr. Litchfield or Mr. Stafford' he wrote:

> thear is one thing that I am not serton weather I menshened but I have thought it most properest to cumenecate to you. thear was to have been small Detachements plased at Diferant Enterenesses in and out of London to prevent Goverment for sending Despatches to haney part of the Cuntrey.
>
> as thear was onely one hors soulger sent with them it would be easey taken from im and then we should know wot steps Goverment was taking and then we should be able to gard against them and the soulger was to be forced to join or taken presener if he would not take the ofer made to im to take the fresh Bountey.
>
> This was proposed by young Watson and thiselwood and a greed to by all
>
> Sir I remain your obeedent servant
John Castle

Before 18 February, when the Government put a price on his head, Thistlewood had had no difficulty in lying low in London; Blood Money hunters were interested only in finding Young Watson, who weighed £500. With his wife and son the Head General moved from one cheap lodging to the next, mainly in Marylebone and Holborn, under various false names. From 18 February onwards, however, safe hiding-places became much

---

*It has been estimated that a total of over half the seats in the Commons were in the gift of about 200 landowners.

harder to find; to make matters worse, in early spring it was strongly rumoured that Young Watson had reached America. Every police nose and informer in London was on the lookout for Arthur Thistlewood, would-be President of the English Republic, last seen escaping from the Horse Patrol at Highgate, and known to be armed. It seemed likely that he would try to follow Jem Watson to America, and the Alien Office was told to make the strictest examination of all persons embarking for that country at British ports.

They had not long to wait. Towards the end of April 1817, a lady travelling in Susan Thistlewood's maiden name of Wilkinson went aboard the American ship *Perseus* at Gravesend, accompanied by a young boy. Soon afterwards three men arrived at Grays, on the opposite side of the Thames estuary, hired a boatman to take them across to Northfleet, and walked into Gravesend along the deserted sea wall.

Before the *Perseus* could be cleared for departure her passengers had to appear before an Inspector aboard the Alien Department brig *Flamer*. On 27 April, with darkened hair and whiskers, wearing a large padded coat to thicken his figure, Thistlewood boarded the *Flamer* and tried to pass himself off as John Wilkinson, farmer. When the Inspector asked him if that was his real name, he insisted that it was.

'It will not do, Mr. Thistlewood,' he was told. 'You are under arrest.'

Though carrying a dirk, Thistlewood made no resistance, and according to *Bell's Weekly Messenger* looked very dejected. Conveyed up the Thames to London, he was landed at Whitehall Stairs the next day, and taken before Lord Sidmouth for examination.

Except for Young Watson, all the alleged leaders of the plot were now in custody – Thistlewood, Doctor Watson, Preston, Hooper and Keens. The Government decided to try them for high treason. To some legal experts this seemed rather unwise; Sir Samuel Romilly, an authority on criminal law and a former Solicitor-General, believed that the charge should have been incitement to riot.

The first step was to convince the Grand Jury for Middlesex, which found true bills for high treason against all the prisoners except Keens. A judge had explained to the Grand Jury members that levying war against the King did not necessarily involve a regular, organised force, nor did the participants have to be in military array. 'If there is an insurrection, that is a large rising of people, by force or violence to accomplish or avenge not any private objects of their own, but to effectuate any general public purpose, that is considered by the Law as a Levying of War.'

The four accused were committed to the Tower. The charge of high treason seemed to have had very little effect on Thomas Preston, who described himself as perfectly serene during his imprisonment, largely because a fortune teller at Brentford had once told him that no prison would ever hold him for long, and that his enemies would make him a great man. In a pamphlet published later in 1817* he wrote :

> The wardors or beef-eaters occasionally excited my risibility; on one occasion they had a very serious quarrel concerning their dinner, and I verily thought they were about to use those weapons on themselves which was intended only to intimidate me. I wrote some poetic lines on the subject, which I shortly intend to publish. It will be entitled Plumb-pudding or the Royal Gorger's Holiday.

Soon afterwards the Home Office approached Richard Heywood, chief witness to the incident on Tower Hill, when the man with the cutlass had shouted at the Guardsmen and offered them double pay. Heywood was asked if he would identify someone suspected of being 'the person who had summoned the Tower'. When he agreed he was taken to the Tower and shown into a room which contained only two men, one of whom was Thistlewood. The other was a Yeoman Warder in uniform.

*   *   *

The trials were scheduled to begin on 9 June. This date had a

* The Life and Opinions of Thomas Preston, Patriot and Shoemaker.

very special significance for Home Office officials, and not merely because of the Spa Fields Gang: they had been warned about it by a Government spy who was touring the North and Midlands, assessing the areas whose main industries, such as weaving and framework-knitting, had been badly hit by the growing use of machines. His findings seemed to bear out Thistlewood's opinion, as quoted by Castle, that the English people were ripe for Revolution.

A good deal of secrecy surrounded this spy, whom Government files referred to simply as 'O'. According to a list which the Treasury Solicitor kept of his movements, on 26 May 'O' was at Derby, where he was told by 'a delegate from the North' that everything would be ready for 9 June. On 28 May Hiley Addington* wrote, 'All our accounts concur in representing the certainty of a general rising in the course of ten days or a fortnight.'

Sure enough, on 8 June a few hundred men collected at three places in Yorkshire, mainly at Engine Bridge near Huddersfield, but dispersed before any real damage was done. The following day a framework-knitter named Jeremiah Brandreth, alias the Nottingham Captain, mustered fifty men in Derbyshire's Wingfield Park and led them towards Nottingham. He believed that the city had already been captured by Revolutionary forces, and that the People's Army, in which he would be head of a division, was going into action all over England. On the march towards Nottingham his men broke into farmhouses to obtain guns and recruits, and one farm servant was shot dead.

At the approach of a small force of cavalry the insurgents fled, and Brandreth went into hiding with a price of £100 on his head. He was captured at Bulwell six weeks later.

---

* Parliamentary Under-Secretary to the Home Office 1812-18.

4

A Brothel Keeper and the Crown

ON THE day that Brandreth led his men towards Nottingham, the Spa Fields Gang were taken by coach to Westminster Hall, where the proceedings began with the trial of Watson. He looked 'genteel in black, his white neck-cloth carefully tied in a horse collar with a barrel knot'. He was allowed to sit facing his judges, with his counsel seated on his right and the Lieutenant-Governor of the Tower on his left. Behind him stood his three fellow prisoners. Hooper and Preston also wore black. Thistlewood, rather more dashing, had on a coloured neck-cloth and blue jacket.

The number of Crown witnesses totalled 250, of whom at least two had seen the summoning of the Tower on 2 December. The first, an accomptant named Merrett, was sure that the man who had shouted at the Guardsmen was neither Watson nor Thistlewood,* and had made a statement to that effect before the Chief Magistrate at Bow Street. He was not called to give evidence at Watson's trial.

The second witness to the incident was Richard Heywood, the man who had been taken to the two-man identity parade in the Tower, and whose evidence was suspect. The defence produced four men who knew Heywood: three of them called him a liar and the fourth described him as a rogue.

An equally dubious witness for the Crown was Vincent Dowling, the shorthand writer who had eavesdropped on Watson and his visitors in Coldbath Fields. At the December rally in Spa Fields he had made a complete record of the Doctor's speech

---

* It was probably Thomas Preston, although there was a rumour that the man who summoned the Tower was a weaver who was never traced.

under conditions which other shorthand writers rated almost impossible. In cross-examination defence counsel asked him :

Q. Have you ever applied for any employment under Government?
A. I have not.
Q. Of any kind?
A. No.
Q. Who desired you to attend on the second of December?
A. I attended by desire of the proprietors of the *Observer* newspaper.
Q. Had you any direction from anyone in the Secretary of State's office, or any magistrate?
A. I had not, nor never had any previous communication with them . . .
Q. Having taken this note on the second of December, to whom did you give the copy when you transcribed it from your note?
A. I gave it to Mr. Beckett.
Q. Mr. Beckett the Under-Secretary of State?
A. Yes, so I understand.

When Jack Castle took the stand he was asked if he had ever seen Preston or Hooper on horseback :

A. No, they both told me they could not ride.
Q. But they were to be generals of division?
A. Yes . . .
Q. Preston cannot ride?
A. He has told me so himself.
Q. And he is lame?
A. Yes.
Q. How was this lame general to lead on his division?
A. He said he could walk fast enough on an occasion of that kind.
Q. He was to have the command of one entire division?
A. Yes, he was.

Castle's unsavoury past had been skilfully researched. He admitted that he had lived at a brothel run by Mother Thoms in King Street, Soho, where his name was still on the doorplate, and that he had been involved with a man named Daniel Davis, who was tried at Guildford in 1812 for forging Bank notes.

Q. The same accident happened at Guildford as upon this occasion?

A. Yes, it did.

Q. Namely, that you were committed upon a charge, and afterwards became a witness against the persons committed upon the same charge?

A. Yes, it did.

At this point counsel's tone changed 'most emphatically and forcibly'.

Q. What became of the man against whom you was a witness?

A. He suffered the laws of his country.

Q. Did he die upon the scaffold as a victim?

A. I was informed he did.

Q. Have you a doubt that he did?

A. No, I have not.

Q. When was this transaction, Mr. Castle?

A. About three or four years ago.

Q. What was the name of this unfortunate man?

A. Davis.

Q. At whose suit were you committed?

A. At the suit of the Bank of England.

Q. Did you make any and what bargain with the Bank of England, before you were permitted as a witness?

A. No, I did not.

Q. Had you no promise of pardon there for being a witness against the man that was hung?

A. None whatever.

With this exchange the defence had scored what barristers of the period called 'a good smart hit', for it was widely believed that the Bank of England used *agents provocateurs* to trap people into passing forged notes, which was a capital offence. It only remained to tie Castle in with Bow Street.

Q. I suppose your person is pretty well known to the police officers?

A. I do not know.

Q. Have you a doubt of it?

A. I do not know; there is only two or three know me.

Q. Why did you change your name?

A. It was my own choice.

Q. You stated that you were in very great distress before February last?

A. Yes, I was.

Q. Who has supported you since your arrest and commitment? You are well dressed now; who has paid for your clothes?

A. I have been supported in Coldbath Fields prison – I mean Tothill Fields.

Q. Who paid for your dress?

A. Mr. Stafford.

Q. How long have you had that coat on?

A. A month or six weeks.

Q. Did Stafford order it for you?

A. No.

Q. Who did?

A. I ordered it at the clothes shop.

Q. Who paid for it?

A. Mr. Stafford.

Q. Ever since your arrest you have been supported by him?

A. I do not know who paid the expenses; the clothes were purchased by Mr. Stafford and given to me.

Q. Have you had any pocket money from Mr. Stafford?

A. I have.

Q. Who furnished the money for your wife's going down to Yorkshire?

A. Mr. Stafford.

A good hanging speech was made by the Solicitor-General, Sir
Robert Gifford, but it was eclipsed by the one made for the
prisoner by Charles Wetherell.[4] On the charge of levying war
against the King he observed :

There was a meeting at Spa Fields; there was a pound of
ammunition; there was one pistol and one sword; speeches
were made. In the march of this army a flagstaff was taken
from two of the five generals; Mr. Stafford routed the main
division; Sir James Shaw, without any arms and without
fear, dispersed the rest of these insurgents. This was the
Attorney-General's civil war.

The ammunition was not a very convincing piece of evidence.
It was hardly credible that it would have been left at Spa Fields
for the police to find, and was almost certainly planted in the
waggon in which it was discovered.

Finally, there was Castle.

'Gentlemen,' Wetherell asked the jury, 'will you suffer four
human beings to be immolated upon the evidence of that *indes-
cribable* villain?'[5]

According to the Attorney-General's son, 'the epithet appeared
so applicable to the mixed infamy of the witness that it struck
upon the sympathies of all.'*

*   *   *

On Monday 16 June, with the hall packed to the doors and a
huge crowd standing outside, Doctor Watson was set to the bar
and Lord Chief Justice Ellenborough began his summing-up.
'You cannot but feel' he told the jury,' that you have had laid before you a body of cogent evidence in proof of the design, charged
against the prisoner, to over-set the Laws and Government of the
country.'

The jury retired at five and came back at twenty-five to seven.
As the Clerk of the Crown Office rose to address them 'a breath-
less anxiety prevailed'.

* Henry John Shepherd, *Memoir of the Right Honourable Samuel Shepherd*, 1841.

MR. BARLOW : Is James Watson Guilty of the High Treason whereof he stands indicted, or Not Guilty?

FOREMAN : Not Guilty.

('*Acquitted*!' shouted a man at the main door to the crowd in New Palace Yard.)

MR. BARLOW : Did he fly for it?*

FOREMAN : I do not understand the question. Do you mean for our verdict?

MR. JUSTICE BAYLEY : Did he fly away from justice?

FOREMAN : No, no.

MR. BARLOW : Gentlemen of the Jury, you say that he is Not Guilty : so you say all, and that is your verdict?

FOREMAN : Yes.

LORD ELLENBOROUGH : The prisoner may be discharged.

DOCTOR WATSON : I wish to observe –

LORD ELLENBOROUGH : No, you had better not.

Watson's acquittal meant that the Crown case against his friends had collapsed. The following day Thistlewood, Preston and Hooper were brought from the Tower and set to the bar. No evidence was called against them, and the Lord Chief Justice directed the jury to find them not guilty.

Sir Samuel Romilly believed that if the defendants had been kept in Newgate instead of the Tower, indicted for a very aggravated riot instead of high treason, and tried at the Old Bailey rather than Westminster Hall, their conviction would have been certain.

There was still a reward of £500 out for Young Watson, and for anyone who had harboured him, but the Home Office was satisfied that he had escaped from England in a ship called the *Venus* – as indeed he had. In view of his singular escape, many people thought of him as quite a daredevil figure; however an Englishman who met him at Pittsburgh that autumn found him short in stature, mean in appearance, and rather stupid. He was employed by a school at a salary of £50 a year.†

---

* Attempting to 'fly' from a charge of treason was a separate offence.

† Henry Bradshaw Fearon, *Sketches of America*, 1818.

For the Crown and its servants, the trials had been a humiliating fiasco, but at least Bow Street had made its customary profit. The £500 reward for Thistlewood's capture was duly paid to the Chief Magistrate, who distributed it amongst the officers concerned. For his services at Doctor Watson's trial, John Stafford was awarded £300.

Not surprisingly, Stafford was detested by Thistlewood and his fellow dissidents. The Chief Clerk had made so many enemies that his home address was kept secret, as a precaution against would-be assassins. On the frequent occasions his name appeared in the list of Crown witnesses at criminal trials, his address was given as 'Bow Street Public Office'.

The hatred which Stafford inspired in London's Jacobins had its origin in the strange case of Colonel Despard, who had planned to kill the King and take over London in 1802. Despard and his group, which included a number of Guardsmen, met chiefly in taverns in Lambeth and Southwark, and these lay in the area covered by Union Hall Public Office. All Despard's plans were betrayed by one of his men, a Grenadier named Thomas Windsor, who made his reports to Stafford, at that time Chief Clerk to the Union Hall magistrates. In November 1802 Stafford led a strong force of police to the Oakley Arms in Lambeth, and arrested the Colonel and over thirty of his men. They made virtually no resistance. Windsor turned king's evidence, and in 1803 Despard and six others were publicly hanged at Horsemonger Lane Gaol. Their corpses were decapitated with an axe, and the dripping heads held up in front of the crowd, estimated at 20,000, which had turned out to watch.[6]

Greatly impressed by Stafford's courage and efficiency, the Chief Magistrate of the day persuaded him to move to Bow Street.

5

The Spies of Bow Street

THE TRIAL and acquittal of the Spa Fields Gang put an end to
Thistlewood's first plot. In the view of the Scottish informer Alex
Richmond, plotting a revolution with Thistlewood's resources
was like trying to capture the fortress of Gibraltar from a
fishing boat.* Other contemporaries, their judgment clouded
by hatred of the Government, saw Thistlewood as the victim of
a subtle Tory conspiracy to restrict the vote; they claimed that
Thistlewood was merely a pawn in the game, in which extremists
were being urged on to violence by *agents provocateurs* so as to
discredit the whole Reform movement. In 1817 Shelley wrote:

> It is impossible to know how far the higher members of
> the Government are involved in the guilt of their infernal
> agents . . . But this much is known, that so soon as the
> whole nation lifted up its voice for parliamentary reform,
> spies went forth. These were selected from the most worthless
> and infamous of mankind, and dispersed among the
> multitude of famished and illiterate labourers. It was their
> business, if they found no discontent, to create it. It was
> their business to find victims, no matter whether right or
> wrong.†

According to *The Times,* a Government spy named William
Oliver had deliberately stirred up the trouble in Derbyshire and
Yorkshire, and had duped Brandreth into action by saying that
70,000 men were ready to rise in London. The *Leeds Mercury*

* Alex Richmond, *Narrative of the Condition of the Manufacturing Population,* 1825.
† The Hermit of Marlowe [P. B. Shelley], *We Pity the Plumage but Forget
the Dying Bird,* 1817.

claimed that 'this hired spy was not only the original contriver, but the only efficient agent in the plot'. It declared that Oliver should be brought to trial. When questions about Government spies and informers were asked in Parliament, one peer elaborated on the allegations in *The Times*. Most of the recent disturbances, he said, had been 'whipped up by the arts of Government emissaries'. Amid the Government's denials, Oliver's name cropped up again, this time defended by the Prime Minister himself. Addressing the House of Lords, Lord Liverpool said that Oliver had rendered 'the most essential services to Government'.

Formerly a sergeant in the Whitechapel Volunteers, the tall and personable Oliver had been in the Fleet Prison for debt from May to October 1816. He was supposed to have told a Dewsbury bookseller that he belonged to a Committee of Five which had arranged Young Watson's escape, and according to a pamphlet on Government spies had been mixed up in Colonel Despard's plot – 'having dexterously contrived to go out at one door as the officers were coming in at another.'*

He was not the only one accused of being an *agent provocateur*. It was even rumoured that Castle had been a spy since the autumn of 1816, and that he had joined the Spenceans on Home Office orders, his main task being to ensure that Hunt was implicated with eccentrics and extremists like Watson and Thistlewood. The evidence disproves this theory : Castle did not become a spy until 1817.[7]

*   *   *

The month after his release Thistlewood wrote to the Home Secretary about the distress which his arrest had caused him. First, he had bought passages to America for himself and his family, together with provisions for the voyage. Secondly, his wife had been put to some expense while he was in custody, and he estimated the sum due to him on these two counts as £180. Thirdly, certain articles had been taken from him and never returned, including a quantity of goose quills, his son's drawing materials, and a bed. Henry Hobhouse, who had just succeeded John Beckett as Permanent Under-Secretary at the

* *Spies and Bloodites!!*, 1817.

Home Office, replied that these claims were wholly inadmissible.

It seems incongruous that the aspiring President of England should be trying to recover £180 from the Government he intended to overthrow, but Thistlewood was short of money. He could barely afford to treat a follower to a glass of rum, let alone finance a revolution. A number of fund-raising ideas had been considered and rejected, such as soliciting a donation from one of Bonaparte's brothers in America or getting a letter of introduction to some rich Frenchman. There was even vague talk of the Queen of Holland as a possible source of support.

Thistlewood wrote two more letters to Lord Sidmouth in August and another in September, mentioning several points which had earlier slipped his mind, such as the fact that Nicholls the thief taker had confiscated his knife and razor. Lord Sidmouth ordered all Thistlewood's possessions, with the exception of the razor, to be returned to him.

Another of the group, too, was writing to Lord Sidmouth. Preston, at a meeting in September, read out the text of a letter which he had composed, but several of the company said that it went too far and advised him not to send it. 'Oh, it's too late now,' he told them, 'for it's been gone about a month.' Not content with that, he suggested that a snuff-box might be made, decorated with such revolutionary symbols as the head of Charles I and an axe. He saw it as a suitable present for the Prince Regent.

There were now five police officers and at least three spies keeping watch on Thistlewood, whose meetings that autumn were held chiefly in East London taverns – the Waterman's Arms or the Knave of Clubs in Bethnal Green, the Crooked Billet in Kingsland Road, the White Swan in Gravel Lane. Occasionally they would assemble at Thistlewood's lodgings at 40 Stanhope Street, Clare Market, or at Preston's house, but they suspected that both these places were watched by the police.

The spies were referred to in Government files by letters of the alphabet and were not supposed to sign their reports. When they did so, their signatures were erased or cut out. One of James

Hanley's reports in the Public Record Office is marked 'Found with the signature torn off, March 1854'.[8] Hanley, of 112 Whitecross Street, was Spy 'A', and reported to Henry Litchfield, the Treasury Solicitor, at Lincoln's Inn. Preston's behaviour astounded him : in Hanley's opinion Preston was 'a fitter object for a madhouse now than a prosecution'. Spy 'B' was an Irishman named John Shegoe who lived in Southwark, reporting direct to Sir Nathaniel Conant at Bow Street. He was quite an educated man, to judge from his ornate hand and correct, if rather pompous, phrasing. ('I have made it a rule not to trouble you, Sir, with any communication relative to the Disaffected unless there was the appearance of immediate danger from their machinations.') He rarely reported anything of value, though he claimed to be a member of Thistlewood's 'Secret Committee of Seven'. No friendly advice, he said, could make any impression on Thistlewood and his associates, whom nothing could stop until they had arrived 'under the gallows tree'.

Doctor Watson would probably have agreed. Thoroughly shaken by his ordeal of standing trial for high treason, he had decided that Spencean aims ought to be accomplished by peaceful means and he was reluctant to involve himself in schemes of violence. According to Preston, he was afraid of getting himself hanged.

Spy 'C' was an interesting case, an ordinary man caught up in the toils of the would-be great. John Williamson, alias Williams, had been a naval seaman in the war and had served as coxswain to Sir Richard Strachan. In the autumn of 1817 he was living in a court off Fleet Street, Bethnal Green, and working as a trimming weaver. At the beginning of September a man asked him if he would join in a rising which was due to start on the last day of Bartholomew Fair. Williamson reported this to the Governor of the Bank of England, who passed him on to the Home Office, where he was persuaded to continue giving information.

Shegoe, too, had got wind of the plot. He wrote to Sir Nathaniel Conant that Thistlewood and Preston were confident of raising 2,000 men.

The Marquis of Wellesley, my lord Grey and others may ridicule and sneer at such an attempt, but I think if they were to know what I know at present of what is going on, and what will be attempted if not counteracted, they would not at public meetings make such speeches as they do . . . Thistlewood is to have a general's uniform by Thursday.

On Saturday, 6 September, he wrote again : 'They will attack the Tower tonight at ten.'

The plan was for Preston, Thistlewood and some others to gather at nine o'clock at the Artillery Ground near Finsbury Square, where they would have a cart filled with pikes and other weapons. These would be issued to recruits hand-picked from the Bartholomew Fair crowd leaving Smithfield. At this period Thistlewood still believed that 40,000 workers would support him in London. The rising would start at ten or eleven, and the first objective would be the Tower armoury. Once that was captured the force would split up. Half the insurgents would take the Bank of England, while the rest would seize the cannon at the Light Horse Drill Hall in Gray's Inn Lane. The ringleaders would meet for supper at the Piebald Horse in Chiswell Street.

On orders from the Home Office, troops were posted at the usual key points, including Gray's Inn Lane and the Bank, Newgate, Whitecross Street Debtors' Prison, and the Giltspur Street Compter. Lord Sidmouth kept in touch with the Lord Mayor, who had received an anonymous warning written on the fifth.

There will be a dreadful massacre tomorrow night. I advise you most earnestly to keep your own, and to cause the children of others to stay at home. Many, many, I assure you, will fall, and the soldiers will certainly join.

Henry Hobhouse kept all the police patrols in town and ordered that, from 6 p.m. on the sixth, each Public Office should be manned by one magistrate and its full strength of constables. Hatton Garden and Worship Street were told to be doubly alert.

Hobhouse himself took post at the Home Office, while the C-in-C Sir Henry Torrens waited at the Horse Guards. At twenty minutes to midnight it began to be apparent that nothing was going to happen. The Lord Mayor was told he could stand down the soldiers at 1 a.m. 'The only alarm,' reported the *Morning Chronicle* tartly, 'was that arising from the appearance of the military in different quarters.'

The plotters had realised that their plans were discovered when they saw that there were soldiers under arms at the Artillery Ground and that the City Police were on the lookout. Preston announced he was so vexed that he could have destroyed himself.

The following month [October 1817] Shegoe reported that twenty-eight men had attended a meeting at the Duke's Arms in Upper Marsh, Lambeth. Thistlewood had told them that the Government no longer seemed to be on its guard, which at least proved that there were no traitors among them. But they must not delay, and must have a signal. One of the group thought that the best signal of all would be to assassinate some famous men – 'that would set all going.'

John Williamson was by now a trusted member of Thistlewood's inner circle, and making regular reports to Henry Litchfield. During his naval service he had been a gunner's mate, which gave him a privileged position with Thistlewood. In the first few hours of the London uprising, cannon would have a vital part to play, and as Thistlewood was no artillerist he needed someone with first-hand knowledge of gunnery to advise him. Williamson was no expert, and his advice was often based on guesswork : when Thistlewood asked whether eight pieces of cannon would make a horse regiment keep its distance, or how many men a nine-pounder shot might kill in the street, Williamson would give the first answer that came into his head. It was lucky that Thistlewood's knowledge of gunnery was so limited – Williamson even had to explain that you looked through the side sight for elevation and used the centre sight for direction of the shot.

Thistlewood rarely discussed any other form of weapon,

though Williamson did hear him say that the pikeheads for the Bartholomew Fair business had been thrown down a sink-hole near Finsbury Square. Apart from the cannon, which could only be acquired once the rising had begun, Thistlewood was interested in money and what he called 'combustibles' – pitch, saltpetre, turpentine and brimstone. These were the ingredients needed to make fireballs which, for the revolutionaries, had a double purpose. By firing the barracks they would knock out the garrisons; and by firing buildings in Spitalfields, Holborn and Southwark they would muster the people, since a good fire was 'the way to get a large mob together'. This was fundamental to any plan. Once they had succeeded in this, they could choose recruits to reinforce the squads detailed to capture the artillery. If he had 400 men at his disposal, Thistlewood confided to Williamson, he could attack any barracks in London and the Tower as well. But, for all his confidence, he spent hours hanging about outside different barracks, trying to discover how many men and cannon they housed and how the sentries were mounted.

One day in October, having failed to elicit enough facts about the Artillery Barracks at Kilburn, he sent Williamson into a tavern used by the gunners with orders to question them. Williamson found the tap room full of soldiers, and when he called for a pint of beer they all turned and stared at him. He went very red and, to cover his embarrassment, asked the nearest corporal whether he knew a man named Smith.

'Smith from what county?' inquired the corporal.

'Warwickshire,' Williamson replied, and explained that, being about to visit Warwickshire, he needed to ask Smith a few questions. The corporal said the only Smith he knew was a Scotsman.

Williamson gulped down his beer and went back to report. Thistlewood asked him how many field pieces there were at the barracks.

'Four,' Williamson replied.

'And the strength of the garrison?'

'Eighty.'

More than satisfied with Williamson for having carried out his orders so promptly, Thistlewood treated him at a public house in

the Tottenham Court Road. The episode was duly reported to
Bow Street by Shegoe, who informed the Chief Magistrate that
Thistlewood now knew the strength of the Kilburn Artillery
Barracks. 'He and Williams are the most sanguinary,' he added.
He also informed Bow Street of Thistlewood's statement that,
'during his stay in Paris, fifty Greeks had puzzled the whole Ger-
man army. 'To what this alludes,' the Chief Magistrate confessed
to Lord Sidmouth, 'I do not recollect.'

*   *   *

Thistlewood planned to attack the Tower on 11 October. Both
Shegoe and Williamson passed on the warning. According to
Shegoe, Thistlewood would station himself outside 14 America
Square at 7 p.m. As soon as 500 men had mustered he would let
off a sky rocket as the signal to begin. He was sure of taking the
Tower, which he said had a garrison of only 400.

On the afternoon of the eleventh Williamson spent some time
closeted with the Treasury Solicitor. In the evening he went to
Tower Hill, only to find that of the thousands expected by
Thistlewood only twelve had actually turned out. Observing
that 'the people were not ripe for it,' Thistlewood took Williamson and a few others into a tavern in Trinity Square. After a few
drinks and a half-hearted conference most of them went quietly
home. The conscientious Williamson, however, walked down to
the Tower and, asking for the Officer of the Guard, told him that
there would be no trouble that night after all. The astonished
officer sent for the Governor, whose first thought was to clap
Williamson into a dungeon. Only when it had been established
that he was vouched for by the Treasury Solicitor was the spy
finally released.

*   *   *

If there were lessons to be learned (and Thistlewood's optimism
made him a poor pupil of events), it was that the insistence on
secrecy made it difficult to assemble a force of any size. Determined that no Government spy should discover his plans until it
was too late to upset them, Thistlewood had adopted a simple
rule : with the exception of a few trusted associates, he never
told anyone what he was going to do until three or four hours before he did it.

It was this obsession with security which led him to change the Oath of Allegiance. In October 1817 there were two oaths in use, one for the Committee members and another for the rank and file. Both laid great emphasis on the need to do one's duty in the cause of liberty. An Other Rank had to swear that if he found a man worthy of trust he would introduce him to the movement. He also undertook to arm himself, be ready to act at a minute's notice, and refrain from asking questions. Thistlewood was becoming increasingly concerned about the security aspects of the oath. He had also decided that his men must have pikes which could outreach the standard infantry musket. He accordingly drafted a revised version of the oath which specified that a man's flesh should be boiled off his bones if he divulged any secrets entrusted to him, and that everyone must equip himself with a pike nine or ten feet long.

Williamson was present when Thistlewood read the oath out to the Committee, which was not much impressed. Thistlewood stressed that it was only a draft and went off to his lodgings to get the Freemason's Oath and 'have it proper', pausing only to write down the names of fifteen men who, he said, could each provide the movement with twenty recruits. One of the fifteen was Shegoe; another was Williamson.

The plan was by now worked out almost to the last detail. As soon as the rising began, the garrisons would be put out of action with fireballs, which would be thrown into barrack rooms and on to the straw in the stables. Drays would be dragged out of the brewery yards and parked across the streets to hamper cavalry. The cannon at the Light Horse Drill Hall and the Artillery Ground would be seized, and if the ones at Gray's Inn Lane could not be brought away they would be spiked. 'Then they would sally down to St. James's Park and soon drive all the soldiers from there.'

Preston would take no part in these excursions, but would take post at St. Giles's. When he heard Thistlewood coming with the field guns he was 'to start up and let all the company know', giving it out that the soldiers from the barracks had joined the mob. For the man who was supposed to have been picked to lead the attack on the Tower in 1816, this was a very minor role. The official reason was that it would be kinder to his lame leg than a more active command. The truth was that, mainly because of Preston's increasingly heavy drinking, Thistlewood could no longer rely on him.

The soldiers at the barracks would be made to harness horses to the guns and perform all their usual tasks except for elevating the guns, which Thistlewood did not trust them to do properly. They would be promised a free discharge, a good pension, and twenty pounds pocket money if they cooperated. Thistlewood's men would stand over them, and run them through with sword or bayonet if they disobeyed orders. There would be spies keeping the insurgents informed of hostile troop movements, especially those of the Life Guards.

Thistlewood was sure that the soldiers in London would join him three or four hours after the rising began; he claimed that they were young men who had been forced to enlist because they had no jobs, and that the Government had demobilised all the veterans who would have been willing to do its dirty work. Some of the replacements who had guarded him in prison, he boasted, would have given him all the help he asked. 'Fifteen Scotchmen in the Third Regiment offered to take me out at any time. There is not four men in the whole Battalion that would hurt me if they were ordered to shoot.'

The 'Piccadilly Butchers', as the Life Guards had been nicknamed in 1810, would need to be 'done over'; after that the other troops would not stand. All the same, it would be prudent to start the rising before 9 p.m. because the garrisons were confined to barracks by that time and could be called out immediately. The best time to start would be seven o'clock.

And so it went on – Thistlewood deploying his imaginary battalions, allocating non-existent resources, solving problems with the utmost dispatch. Cartridges? He had them all ready. Gunpowder? One of them would pose as the captain of a ship and simply buy what they required. Allies? Once the English Republic was proclaimed, there would be another Revolution in France (though they must take care not to act as they did when Boney went into Russia). Ships? Twenty sail of the line would be fitted out; Thistlewood hoped soon to see Williamson an admiral.

Williamson was risking his life by exploiting Thistlewood's trust in this way, and must have known it. He had tried, without success, to persuade the Treasury Solicitor to have him arrested during the projected attack on the Tower; now, in late October, he reported that the massive precautions taken by the authorities that day had convinced Thistlewood that he had a spy in his camp.

Another incident, allied to a prediction, made Williamson even more uneasy. His father-in-law was already warning him not to attend any more meetings, because Williamson's mother had had his nativity cast, and it appeared that Williamson would be in great trouble in his thirty-sixth year (Williamson was then thirty-six).

The incident concerned his friend George Pickard, also an ex-sailor, who was a regular attender at Thistlewood's meetings. A gold lace weaver by trade, Pickard lived at 15 Hare Street, Bethnal Green,* one of the meanest parts of the city. One day that October rather a respectable-looking man called at his house and, when Pickard's wife explained that he was not at home, asked where he might be found. Pickard's wife would not say, but asked the man his name and business. He replied that his name did not matter, but advised her to tell her husband to keep a good lookout for himself, or he would soon be in a hobble.

Williamson concluded that something terrible was about to happen at a meeting, very possibly to himself, for he did not think that Thistlewood's group would hesitate when it came to killing a spy. 'They discoursed upon Castles,' he reported, 'and how they would serve him if they ever met him; they would not mind cutting his entrails out.' Henry Litchfield, however, managed to assure Williamson that his fears were groundless, which was in fact the case. The only members of his circle whom Thistlewood suspected at this period were Shegoe and Doctor Watson.

Williamson had already noticed that Thistlewood never said

* Now Cheshire Street.

much at any meeting where Watson was present. On one occasion Watson showed Thistlewood a threatening letter which he had received; afterwards Thistlewood told Williamson that he believed the letter to be a fake, and that Watson had written it himself. At about the same time, one of the police officers who were watching Thistlewood heard him exclaim, 'Damn Doctor Watson! Look at his milk-and-water letters to Lord Sidmouth when he was in prison. I would never have demeaned myself.'

At the end of the month Shegoe reported on a meeting at Thistlewood's lodgings, in the course of which a man called Pinkerton told him that the Prince Regent and possibly the members of the Privy Council were going to be killed.

It was suggested by Thistlewood that the best way of effecting this infernal and very diabolical proposition was at a Cabinet or publick Dinner. But this was not to be attempted if they had numbers sufficient to undertake a more noble and general enterprize, but as the last resort. I did not get to my bed until three o'clock this morning.

6

Thistlewood Goes to Gaol

JEREMIAH BRANDRETH, the man who had led the abortive march on Nottingham, was tried before a Special Commission at Nottingham, together with a number of men accused of having followed him. On 15 October the Treasury Solicitor ordered Oliver the spy to be sent up from London, travelling under a false name and wearing some sort of disguise. He was lodged at the house of a solicitor but never produced at the trial, which began on 25 October.

Brandreth and two other men were sentenced to death by hanging, the corpses to be decapitated and quartered, but the Regent remitted the quartering when he signed the warrant for the execution, which was carried out at Derby on 7 November. Heavily ironed and crouched on a sledge made by a local joiner, the three men were pulled round the prison yard by a draught horse. Having thus suffered the traitor's fate of being drawn on a hurdle, they were taken out and hanged before a huge crowd. 'This is all Oliver and the Government,' one of the victims declared on the scaffold.

The bodies hung on the gallows for half an hour. After they had been taken down, the heads were cut off and held up while the traitors' names were called out according to custom. The identity of the headsman was kept secret: he was said to be a collier who had been paid twenty-five guineas for his trouble.

The affair had a profound effect on Preston and Thistlewood. 'They are in a state of despair,' Shegoe told Bow Street, 'and know not what to do, because they cannot find sanguinary madmen like themselves to commit murder and destruction.'

Thistlewood told Williamson he was sure that the Government

knew 'all his goings-on', and he expected to be arrested any day; in the meantime he was hoping to profit by the death of young Princess Charlotte, the Regent's only child.[9] A few days after she was buried, he said, there would be 'a bit of a disturbance among the nobs', and he was thinking of posting placards to announce that she had been poisoned by her unnatural father. He lost interest in this scheme when an Irishman offered to introduce him to a gentleman who had 20,000 men organised, 1,000 of them armed. A meeting was arranged, but the Irishman's contact never arrived.

Preston's behaviour was as erratic as ever. He upset several members by announcing that he was moving to Blackfriars Road, on the south side of the Thames. Two of his friends told him they would never attend meetings on the Surrey bank, claiming that juries on that side of the water acted differently from those on the Middlesex side. But Preston explained that it was essential; his house had recently been watched all night by three officers from Bow Street. There was also the reason, not mentioned by Preston but reported to the Home Office by Sir Nathaniel Conant, that he owed twenty pounds to his landlord at Clement's Inn and five pounds in tax. Conant also knew that the move was not to Blackfriars Road, but to Westminster Bridge Road, where Preston was to be found with his four daughters at number three.

There was also a difference between Preston's account of a visit to Birmingham and the confidential account of it from Bow Street. Aware that Preston was going to speak at Reform meetings, Conant had him shadowed by a Runner, who reported that the audiences all gave him a lukewarm reception. Preston, however, was full of the success of his trip. The chairmen of the different meetings, he said, had abandoned their speeches to give him more speaking time, and so many people had turned out to hear him that they could not all be admitted. The mood of the men in Birmingham was excellent; it remained only for London to give them a lead. When he had left, a crowd had gathered to cheer his coach.

Of the original defendants of the Spa Fields Gang, only

Thistlewood and Preston were actively planning Revolution. The Doctor was taking a calmer line; and John Hooper was desperately ill. Hooper's wife, an ex-prostitute, had strong words to say about Thistlewood's sense of loyalty, telling William Westcott of Bow Street that Hooper was lying in St. Thomas's Hospital, and that Thistlewood was the biggest villain in the world for not helping him in his illness. She was prepared to do anything to expose him, she said, and told Westcott that Thistlewood was going about with a short dirk up his sleeve and had a sword in his stick. Furthermore, he was connected with a very mischievous man in Southwark known as 'Tumble Down Dick'.

Hooper died in January 1818. Williamson reported that Thistlewood intended to advertise his funeral on 250 placards and in the newspapers, since he thought that the funeral of a man who had been acquitted of high treason was bound to cause a stir; and as the burial was to be in Stepney Church on a Sunday, thousands of the East End poor would be on the streets. On their way back from the cemetery, Williamson warned, Thistlewood and his men would try to seize the cannon at the Artillery Ground, and attack the Tower Hamlets Arms Depot in Bethnal Green. 'The Leaders of Sedition etc. will *be at the Burial*,' Shegoe added.

Meanwhile the body lay at the premises of Mr. Savidge, a window-blind maker in the New Cut, who was collecting for the funeral expenses and the cost of erecting a stone. 'Hooper's wife (not married to him),' noted Sir Nathaniel Conant, 'is going about to get money which she keeps herself, and is disapproved of.' The body, according to Williamson, would not be moved until 1 p.m. on the day of the funeral, so that it would be dark before everything was over.

In the event, police were posted along the procession route and near the churchyard in such strength that once again Thistlewood cancelled his plans and called a meeting instead. It was held that evening at the Cheshire Cheese in Fleur-de-Lis Court, where Mr. Savidge sang the *Ca ira*.

Later that month, Williamson told Thistlewood that he was

thinking of giving up going to meetings, because Thistlewood was always disappointing him; he felt that if no one was ever going to do anything they might as well all stay at home. Thistlewood explained that his men were afraid to risk their lives because of their families, who would all starve if their menfolk got killed in a revolution. He proposed to start a fund, which could provide for the relatives of any man who lost his life in the cause.

The next meeting, held on 1 February, was very well attended, with between thirty and forty men filling the back room of the Spotted Dog in Clement's Inn Passage. Business had hardly begun when someone announced there was a spy in the room.

Thistlewood asked who was he and where was he sitting? He was told it was 'near the door', whereupon a man at the back rose and said, 'Gentlemen, I suppose you mean me?'

'Yes, by God,' exclaimed the man who had raised the alarm. 'You are a Bow Street officer, and the sooner you are out the better it will be for yourself.' The spy hurried out. A member snatched up Thistlewood's swordstick and went after him, but returned presently to report that the spy had vanished; otherwise, he said, he would have 'given him the contents' of Thistlewood's stick.

Before the meeting could settle down again, Thistlewood got to his feet and denounced Doctor Watson, saying that on his release from the Tower Watson had written to Lord Sidmouth thanking him for favours received. Watson was not the man he professed to be, Thistlewood insisted, or he would never have sent the letter.

Watson happened to have a copy of the letter with him, and after reading it out he tried to explain why he had written it. Lord Sidmouth had granted him several privileges while he was in the Tower and allowed his many friends to visit him. He had considered it only right to thank his lordship and failed to see how this made him any worse a man 'in a political view'.

Thistlewood then challenged Watson to meet him the following Monday with sword or pistol, according to the Doctor's choice, but the other members made them shake hands and drop the matter. Business gradually returned to normal and soon afterwards Preston arrived, saying that he had succeeded in forming three very large sections.

*   *   *

Thistlewood, meanwhile, was still trying to get the Home Office to refund his £180. At the end of January he had written to Lord Sidmouth:

> Multiplicity of business can be no excuse for your not answering my letter of the 24th instant, as you have such a swarm of underlings to do your work. I now write to know when it will suit your convenience to give me an audience, for one I will have, that I may hear from your own lips what excuse you can make for this dastardly barefaced robbery. I am not in a humour to throw away £180.

After waiting two days for a reply he challenged Sidmouth to a duel. 'I leave the choice of sword or pistols to your lordship. As for time, I shall brook of no delay.'

Sidmouth was reluctant to take legal action, feeling that people would assume that he was afraid to meet Thistlewood, but after much argument the Prince Regent and the Cabinet made him see reason. At Sidmouth's suit, Thistlewood was removed to the King's Bench Prison. Found guilty of causing a breach of the peace he was sentenced to twelve months' imprisonment, and entered Horsham Gaol on 28 May 1818.

Horsham was one of the prisons which earned a good report from John Howard, who found it clean and well run, but Thistlewood thought it most unsatisfactory, mainly because of the overcrowding and the excessively strict discipline. At the end of June he wrote to Sidmouth saying that it was truly disgusting for two or three men to sleep in a cell measuring nine feet by seven, and asked to be transferred to Maidstone or Winchester. He said after his release that he preferred the Tower.

Having spent some time discussing their sentences with eight other prisoners, who were all well-known smugglers, he wrote to inform the Home Office that they had been wrongly imprisoned and ought to be released. At about the same time he learned that a Lincolnshire acquaintance named John Hunt had been to see his wife and offered to look after young Julian. He immediately wrote to Hunt about what he called these clandestine visits to 40 Stanhope Street, and accused him of trying to entice away his son. 'I can prove by receipts,' he ended, 'that he has cost me Three Hundred Pounds; if you have it in your power to refund that, and if it is Julian's wish to go with you, I should not refuse him, but only regret his folly.'

£300 just happened to be the amount of personal bail which Thistlewood would have to find when his sentence expired; in addition, he needed to obtain two other sureties, each of £150 for three years. The two men who had originally agreed to stand surety for him had gone to America, and no one else seemed anxious to step into the breach. This was a serious matter, because until Thistlewood could find two more sureties he would not be released. In London a rumour began to circulate that Mrs. Thistlewood was putting all the blame for this on Doctor Watson, and saying that he had been telling people not to go bail for her husband. Watson wrote her a curt letter demanding that she tell him who had invented this calumny. 'If you do not,' he ended, 'you will leave me to conclude that it proceeds from your own unhappy turn for ungrounded suspicion.'

* * *

Since Preston's drinking and instability made him unfit for any real sort of leadership, Thistlewood's removal to Horsham left Watson the undisputed leader of London's Spenceans, though the name was no longer used. 'There was no meeting of the Committee last Thursday,' wrote Williamson in one report, 'because Doctor Watson was unable to attend.' Williamson had now been what the Home Office called 'a confidential person' for nearly a year and was much more sure of himself. When Preston wanted him to join in a burglary which was being planned to raise funds, Williamson refused point blank, saying that his height made him too conspicuous.

His name still kept cropping up in the reports of his fellow spy John Shegoe, who described him as 'formerly a sailor and one of the Rioters who threw stones at Sir Murray Maxwell and followed and threw dirt at My Lord Castlereagh and was an Aid de Camp of Thistlewood'. In Shegoe's opinion Doctor Watson and his circle were a set of the greatest miscreants that ever disgraced society. 'As they are desperate wicked men who would engage in anything,' he wrote, 'I shall constantly watch their movements night and day until they are counteracted.'

In point of fact Shegoe's value as a spy, which had never been very high in London, was at its lowest point. At a meeting in June, Williamson reported, Doctor Watson announced that a clerk in one of the public offices had warned him that Shegoe was a spy, who had worked for the Government in France and Ireland and drawn a pension of £6 a month ever since.

'Damn his blood,' said a weaver, 'I suspected him a good while.' The meeting resolved that Shegoe was 'a Suspected Person'.

Watson was anxious not to provoke the Establishment, which he considered much too strong to be overthrown by force. In London, the Household troops alone numbered at least 4,000 men.[10] When someone asked Watson how he proposed to achieve Radical reform if not by force, he replied that he did not know, but time would tell.

In John Stafford's opinion, Watson's meetings were Spencean in all but name, though the spy James Hanley declared, more dramatically, 'These infatuated men had fully persuaded themselves of their competency to rule the nation.' According to Hanley, Watson had two main problems: the disappearance of Spa Fields, which had been largely built over since 1816, and the shortage of money. For a rally in September it was decided to use Palace Yard, and a collection of £5 was taken up in advance to cover expenses. Watson said that this was not nearly enough, because the placards giving notice of the meeting would cost £7 to begin with.

In an unusual mood of caution, Preston told the Committee that they were taking a risk in collecting subscriptions as they did, because there was an Act of Parliament called the Combination Act which forbade it. No one paid much heed to this, and a carpenter was told to make twelve collecting boxes for the Palace Yard meeting at a cost of one shilling and ninepence each. Hanley was present at the Falcon in Fetter Lane when the boxes were opened after the meeting, and was able to report that the contents totalled £1-13-6¾d.

*   *   *

On 23 November Watson warned the meeting at the George in East Harding Street that a Government spy was present, and pointed him out. The man got up and admitted that he belonged to Bow Street, but claimed to be as sympathetic towards a reform of Parliament as anyone present; furthermore, he said, he had paid his subscriptions regularly, so if anyone offered violence towards him he would knock him down. This resulted in much hissing and shouts of 'Castle! Oliver!', but the Bow Street man said that insult would not keep him away; he would come and smoke his pipe and drink his pint whenever he felt like it. However, he left soon afterwards and John Stafford decided that it would be dangerous to send him again.

At this period there were at least eight men spying on Watson and his meetings, including Williamson, Shegoe, Hanley, an official of the Alien Office, an informer referred to as 'B.C.', and several police officers. In 1818 there was a new recruit, a man whom Bow Street referred to as 'W - - - r'. One of his reports was written on the back of a letter addressed to a London shopkeeper, asking him to sell busts of the Princess Elizabeth on a commission of twenty-five per cent. The letter was signed 'George Edwards, modeller, Eton, near Slough'.

7

'The Boy for Doing Business'

In 1819, as in the 1970s, the buildings of Gray's Inn Lane were an odd mixture, especially at the southern end. On one side were the handsome quadrangles of Gray's Inn, on the other the squalid dwellings which lined Portpool Lane, Liquorpond Street, Baldwin's Gardens and Fox Court. It was at 4 Fox Court that John Thomas Brunt lived with his wife and son.

Undersized and rather ugly, Brunt was an intelligent man and a voracious reader, whose favourite authors were Paine and Voltaire. A boot-closer by trade, he had travelled on the Continent, working for the British Army in France and Belgium. He rented two rooms on the second floor at number four, using one room to live in and the other for his work.

In Regency London the members of the boot-making trade all seemed to know one another, and Brunt was on Christian-name terms with clickers and cloggers in hovels and tenements as far away as Marylebone. He was good at his job, and had once been able to earn forty or fifty shillings a week; but like most of his fraternity he found it hard to make ends meet in the post-war depression, and in 1819 sometimes had to exist on ten shillings a week. Luckily he had a good friend in the person of George Edwards.

Brunt had met him at the White Lion in Wych Street, that part of Old London, full of Jacobean buildings, at the end of Drury Lane. Edwards used to call at 4 Fox Court several times a day; if Brunt was not at home, he would wait for him. He even went with him to his customers' houses, which sometimes proved embarrassing, especially when a client spotted Edwards hanging about outside, and Brunt had to explain who he was. From time to time Edwards gave Brunt money and paid him compliments, saying that if only he could get a hundred men like Brunt, there was nothing he would not be able to accomplish. 'He often took me out to call on people,' Brunt testified, 'and to treat them with drink. From the different favours I received from Edwards, I had a good opinion of the man.'

Others were less keen on George Edwards and his pushing ways. At the White Lion one evening Edwards got into conversation with a bootmaker named Thomas Chambers and discovered that he lived at 3 Heathcock Court, off the Strand. To Chambers's surprise, since he hardly knew the man, Edwards called on him soon afterwards and talked politics in 'a strange, violent manner'. On a second visit he told Chambers that 'it was nonsense talking, people must arm themselves'. He seemed to think that everyone should be as hostile to the Government as he was himself, and ought to make no bones about saying so. He had an unnerving trick of pulling a hand grenade from his pocket and asking a man what he thought about it. He referred quite frequently to Lord Castlereagh, though not always in the same strain, one day boasting that his lordship had helped him claim a legacy, the next insisting that 'the bloody Irish butcher must be made away with'.

On one occasion, when he brought several strangers to call on Chambers, including two drunken Irishmen, Edwards had a swordstick in his hand and an old cavalry sword under his coat. He asked one of the Irishmen, 'Would you not wish to have Castlereagh's head to carry about on a pole, for the good he has done your country?'* The Irishman agreed that Castlereagh was a big rogue, at which Edwards pulled out his sabre, saying, 'Here is what will cut off his bloody head.'

When one of the men said that he would never enter into anything until he was sworn, Edwards promptly asked for a Bible with which to swear him. This was too much for Chambers, who bundled them all out, and he was much annoyed when Edwards called again the following week and delivered another tirade against the Government.

---

* Son of an Ulster landowner, Castlereagh had been Secretary for Ireland during the Irish Rebellion of 1798. In 1819 he was Foreign Secretary.

Another man who knew Edwards in 1819 was George Pickard, the Bethnal Green weaver and friend of Williamson. During a discussion on politics, Edwards remarked to Pickard that it would be very easy to assassinate Members of Parliament in the House of Commons, provided one went the right way about it. The first step was to cut up a number of old gun and pistol barrels into pieces about three inches long, fill the centres with gunpowder, plug the ends with lead, and bore a touch-hole. They could then be packed into half a dozen iron cases made to look like books, which six men could easily take into the House of Commons.

> One man might have a bottle of phosphorus, and a lighted match might be taken with a piece of rope, without giving any alarm, and applied to the fuse, which would communicate with the contents of the cases.*

If the cases could be thrown from the Commons gallery into a full Chamber, said Edwards, 'what bloody destruction it would make.' After some further talk he drew out a hand grenade, saying that Thistlewood would soon be out of prison, and *he* was 'the boy for doing business'. When Thistlewood came out, said Edwards, he would 'set all things to rights'.

Edwards seemed to make a point of cultivating men who had come down in the world – 'men who had once enjoyed a comparative state of affluence; and comparing past with present became dissatisfied, arguing with themselves that whatever might be the consequences of the step which they were going to take, their situation could not be worse.'†

James Ings, an out-of-work butcher, was a good example. He had once owned some slum property in his home town of Portsea, but trade was so bad at the end of the war that in 1819 he sold his tenements and moved to London. He first opened a butcher's shop, then a coffee shop in Old Montague Street, Whitechapel. When both these ventures failed, he sent his wife

---

* Edward Aylmer, *The Memoirs of George Edwards,* 1820.
† ibid.

and children to stay with friends in Portsmouth; at the time Edwards met him he was living alone in poor lodgings at Primrose Street, Bishopsgate. Edwards took him under his wing, treated him in public houses, and gave him money. Unlike Brunt, who knew journeymen shoemakers all over London and read Voltaire, Ings had no contacts and very little brain. It was hard to know what use the shrewd and fiery Edwards had for this penniless Hampshire butcher. His Irish friends, had anyone asked them, might have joked about it being something to do with Castlereagh's head.

In due course Brunt introduced Edwards to his friend and neighbour Richard Tidd, a Lincolnshire-born man of about forty-five. During the war he had been a bounty jumper, joining up under a false name and deserting as soon as his bounty had been paid; he was said to have enlisted in half the regiments under the Crown. The father of eight children, he lived at 5 Hole-in-the-Wall Passage, a slum alley running off Baldwin's Gardens, Gray's Inn Lane. He was earning quite good money as a shoemaker.

It was through George Edwards, who was acquainted with Preston, that Brunt, Ings and Tidd became involved with Thistlewood.

*   *   *

Thistlewood's sentence expired on 28 May, but because of the trouble over his sureties his release was put back for several days. Early in June 1819 he returned to 40 Stanhope Street, and was introduced to George Edwards at Preston's house soon afterwards.

He had changed a lot in his year at Horsham. At the time of Watson's trial in 1817 the papers had described him as a stout, active, cheerful-looking man, with a determined expression and rather devil-may-care air. In 1819 he was much thinner, almost emaciated and, though still active and determined, anything but cheerful. He was often seen hurrying through the streets of Holborn and the City, a slim, dark-haired man with a long face and sallow complexion, shabbily dressed in a blue greatcoat and pantaloons. Yet with Preston and his kind Thistlewood's reputation had never been higher. Here was a veteran of five or six revolutions, an ex-officer turned Republican, and a fine swordsman : a man who had seen the French Revolution at first hand, endured the ordeal of imprisonment in the Tower, and challenged the Home Secretary to a duel.

For the first three months after his release, Thistlewood's favourite haunt was the White Lion in Wych Street, which was close to his lodgings in Stanhope Street. Approached by a narrow passage about thirty yards long, the White Lion was rather a sinister place.

In the tap-room, over the embers of an expiring fire, sat a set of suspicious, ill-looking fellows, huddled close together; whilst at a small deal table to the right sat Mr. ———, with a book and some papers and printed bills before him; from the obscurity of the place, having no light but what proceeded from a candle placed before Mr. ———, or from that in the bar, a stranger coming in would not be able to recognise any of the faces on seeing them afterwards elsewhere. On the right hand, on entering the house, is a small parlour; here of an evening a select committee assembled, and no others were admitted. This was the room in which the most private transactions were carried on; Mr. Thistlewood or Doctor Watson always came out into the passage to speak to any person who called there on business.*

In Thistlewood's absence, the condition of London's labouring poor had slightly improved, but it was still wretched in the extreme. 'This is to inform your bloody Highness,' warned one anonymous letter to the Regent, 'if you don't adopt some measure to procure some relief for the poor your bloody head shall come off and some other person elected more fit to govern the Country, not such a Gouty Old Bugger as you.'

On 21 July Hunt, Thistlewood and Watson attended a meeting at Smithfield. The Government expected trouble and the

* George Theodore Wilkinson, *An Authentic History of the Cato Street Conspiracy*, 1820.

usual orders were issued to the Life Guards, the Lancers at Hounslow, the London militia and the Public Offices. Nothing happened. Two weeks later, the informer 'B. C.' reported on a gathering at the White Lion, at which a man named Hartley complained about the lack of spirit.

> HARTLEY : You are all Cowards, let us try what can be done with physical force.
> DR. WATSON : It is of no use till the Country is ready. I will lose my life as well as the rest, but till the time comes it is only exposing ourselves.
> THISTLEWOOD (*very seriously*) : We shall all be hanged.

At Thistlewood's words, 'the whole Company laughed heartily'.

To discourage firebrands such as Hartley, the authorities could always put on an impressive show of strength in London when the need arose, but in Manchester the situation was very different. On 24 July a magistrate* wrote to the Home Office from Longsight :

> It is with horror I inform you that Birch the officer, into whose hands Harrison the Reformist was consigned in London, was shot by an Assassin in Stockport and now lies in the most dangerous state . . . Indeed, my Lord, these are most tremendous times. I am not an Alarmist, but I think I foresee in this only a prelude to future Bloodshed . . . From different Quarters I hear the Town of Manchester is to be burnt and plundered in the night – A Colonel of a late Volunteer Corps reports that in his neighbourhood the Pike exercise is performed night and morning, and I have this moment heard from undoubted authority that a Waterloo Medallist has been drilling them.

The future bloodshed was just over three weeks away. On 16 August Hunt addressed the famous meeting in St. Peter's Fields,

---

* Rev. C. Ethelston.

and Yeomanry were sent into the crowd with orders to arrest him. The crowd closed round the horses, until it seemed to the watching magistrates that the Yeomanry were in danger, and the Fifteenth Hussars were sent to their aid.

The exact details of the resulting 'Massacre' are hard to establish; certainly 'Peterloo' was blown up by Radical propagandists, who spoke of corpses being hurriedly buried without an inquest and 600 casualties. The death roll reached eleven, including a man who died some days later from the effects of a sabre cut.

The Peterloo Massacre convinced Thistlewood that the Government's days were numbered. Manchester now had a special significance for Radicals, and Manchester delegates were very popular as speakers at the autumn meetings in London. One of them, a lady named Wilson, claimed to carry two pistols about with her. At a meeting in the White Horse, Turnmill Street, she complained that there was no spirit in London : in Manchester, she said, she could always find both money and arms, but in London 'they were all cowards'. Much to Doctor Watson's dismay, Thistlewood decided that in future all the men in his circle should be armed.

The hero of Peterloo was of course Henry Hunt, who was given a hero's welcome when he entered London on 13 September, sitting in a landaulet drawn by six red-ribboned horses, and followed by chariots bearing Thistlewood, Watson and Preston. A dinner in his honour, held at the Crown and Anchor tavern, was attended by over 200 people.

Mr. Richard Birnie watched some of the proceedings from the Music Gallery and sent a report to the Home Office. 'Some busy fool informed Hunt that I was in the Gallery, so he began of course to attack the police and I came away.' He added that the toasts were drunk chiefly in water : 'you never saw so contemptible a crew.'

Birnie was one of the assistant magistrates at Bow Street, and a self-made man. Born in 1760, he had started his working life apprenticed to a saddler in his native Scotland. Moving to London, he went to work for a firm which supplied harness to the

Royal Family, and was sent one day to attend the Prince of Wales. The Prince took a liking to 'the young Scotchman' and it was not long before Birnie was promoted foreman. Later he became a partner in his employer's firm and married a wealthy baker's daughter.

He was a man of many interests. In addition to being a churchwarden and a captain in the Westminster Volunteers he served as a justice of the peace, and by spending long hours listening to what went on at Bow Street court he picked up a working knowledge of a magistrate's duties. He sat on the bench at Union Hall before going to Bow Street. Autocratic, vindictive and widely disliked, he was very ambitious. In 1819 the things which he coveted most in the world were the post of Chief Magistrate and the knighthood that went with it.

*   *   *

The Manchester Massacre had some unexpected results, the oddest being a letter which arrived at Bow Street headed 'My Deare frend Mr. Staford'. The writer enclosed for Stafford's information a few seditious pamphlets which were being sold in 'stashener's shopes' in Sheffield and offered his further services: 'I am serton if I was at Manchester I could be of great serves in finding out those Ring leaders whome wishes to overturn the Conesteutshon and Breek the publick pece.' The letter was signed 'Your most obeedent serveant, John Castle. (Please to Derect G. Smith, Quenes Head, Castle Hill, Sheffield.)'[11]

Another surprising sequel to Peterloo was the rift between Watson and Hunt. According to James Hanley, Watson had put Sir Charles Wolseley's name on the Crown and Anchor dinner tickets without asking Hunt's permission, and this so annoyed Hunt that he behaved towards Watson, in Preston's phrase, 'very despoticly'.

Thistlewood, too, had fallen foul of Hunt, who actually accused him of being a spy. Hunt claimed that a visit of Thistlewood's to Manchester had been subsidised by the Government, and that he had traced the payment for it to the Treasury. According to Alex Richmond, it was well known that Thistlewood had paid for the trip by selling some of his books and pledging others; nonetheless, says Richmond, Hunt's absurd accusation so preyed on Thistlewood's mind that he longed to perform some bold and daring act to give it the lie.* The most convincing act of all would have been to start the London uprising; but that was impossible without money, and Thistlewood was in his usual indigent state.

On 28 September, in surprisingly moderate language, he again asked Lord Sidmouth to pay him back his £180. 'You must be sensible that money is always useful to a poor man,' he wrote, and ended 'I am, my lord, your very obedient servant.' When this plaintive approach failed he reverted to his normal style, and a month later demanded the repayment of his money, plus three years' compound interest, 'out of the candle ends and cheese-parings of your office'.

United by their differences with Hunt, Watson and Thistlewood addressed a rally on 1 November in Finsbury Square, at which Shegoe predicted that there would be 'bloody work'. Mr. Birnie and one of the Thames magistrates watched the proceedings from the Finsbury Coffee House. In a dispatch from the Coffee House, Birnie reported that several flags were being carried, including one inscribed, 'He that hath no Sword, let him sell his garment and buy one'. About 2,000 people had turned out, but only 200 of them seemed to have any interest in the speeches. Birnie remained unimpressed by Thistlewood and his followers, an attitude which the spies did not share. 'Although their numbers are few,' James Hanley observed, 'their Projects are desperate.'

Many magistrates in the North and Midlands expected a rising that autumn, and copies of secret letters written at the time show that Whitehall officials in general, and Henry Hobhouse in particular, were in a tense but determined mood.

As Assistant Treasury Solicitor, Hobhouse had been closely involved in Watson's trial in 1817, and what he did not know about Thistlewood's recent activities and future intentions was hardly worth knowing. Thistlewood's mail was being opened by the Post Office, and John Stafford was transmitting to the Home

* Alex Richmond, op. cit.

Office the reports of half a dozen spies (one of whom reported that Thistlewood had ordered a man to dress up in women's clothing and watch Stafford's house).

Aged forty-two, Hobhouse now had two years' experience as Permanent Under-Secretary behind him. Understandably, his official correspondence at this anxious period is often brusque and admonitory, though his letters to Major-General Sir John Byng are friendly and at times confiding. A Peninsula veteran who had led a Guards brigade at Waterloo, Byng now commanded the Northern district from headquarters at Pontefract. His lucid reports and tempered judgments, especially to a civil servant who had to rely on slow-witted boroughreeves and nervous magistrates, were a godsend. 'It does my heart good to correspond with you,' Hobhouse told him.

Lord Sidmouth was convinced of the need to restrict public meetings, give more power to magistrates, and curb the Radical press, and he was largely responsible for the Government's repressive and highly unpopular Six Acts. As these were due to come into force on 13 December, the Home Office expected Thistlewood to make a move on or before that date. On 27 November Hobhouse told Byng, 'Thistlewood says they must fight for it in less than ten days, and last night sent off Walker to Manchester, from whence he had come as a Delegate, to prepare them there.'

As Thistlewood meant to go to Manchester himself, the local authorities were ordered to keep a close watch on him, but in the end he failed to raise the money for his trip and stayed in London. Hobhouse reported this to Byng on 1 December and added, 'He despairs of the Metropolis, and relies on deliverance by means of the Hordes which are to come down upon us from the North.'

To precipitate action in the North, Hobhouse said, Thistlewood planned to stop the Northern mails leaving London, to give the impression that he was controlling the city. It seemed most unlikely that Thistlewood could capture a mail coach, though it was just possible that a surprise attack might succeed. If any mail coach failed to arrive on time, Hobhouse ordered, the magistrates must do everything necessary to prevent a panic. All the information pointed to serious trouble on 13 December, and writing to Byng on that date he added, 'We look with anxiety for the Posts of to-morrow and Wednesday morning.'

That week, Manchester looked like a town preparing for a siege. The garrison, which already included seven companies of the Eighty-fifth, was reinforced on the thirteenth by a detachment of the Ninth Light Dragoons, and troops of the Cheshire Yeomanry were ready to ride in at the first sign of trouble. The authorities advised all women, children and servants to stay indoors, and in the event of a disturbance well-disposed citizens were asked to put lights in their upper windows. In Glasgow the garrison was under arms from early morning and the volunteer sharpshooters turned out in force.

The day passed off peacefully. Next day Hobhouse informed Byng : 'This morning's mails have somewhat enlivened our Prospect, and I flatter myself that to-morrow's will dispel more of our clouds; for if the commotion does not take place now, I shall almost cease to expect it.' Before he had finished the letter, news arrived that the general commanding the troops in Scotland believed a rising to be imminent, and was moving the whole of his force on Glasgow.

* * *

On 16 December John Williamson made out his last report. There had been meetings every night of the week : at a private house, at the White Lion, and at a public house – newly painted, and lacking a sign – in New Crown Court, off the Strand. To one of these meetings, Hartley and a man named Davidson had brought six cutlasses each, which were given to the men who had no weapons.

On 20 December there was a meeting at Preston's house, and it was attended by Bankes, who was the spy Bow Street referred to as 'B. C.' When it was over, Bankes reported, a man named Williamson followed him out, and advised him not to go to any more meetings, as the others intended to do him some harm. Williamson also told Bankes that Thistlewood and others were planning some desperate act, and as he, Williamson, was determined not to be involved in it, he was going on board ship that very day at Deptford and sailing to the Cape.[12]

This ship was *La Belle Alliance*. Just before he sailed in her, Williamson gave a pawn ticket which he could not redeem to a friend of his, a coloured man from Jamaica named William Davidson. It was for a blunderbuss, in pledge for seven shillings at the pawnshop of James Aldous in Berwick Street, Soho.

8

The Paupers of Fox Court

FORTUNATELY for himself, Doctor Watson had been arrested for debt on 24 November and confined in Whitecross Street Debtors' Prison. On 23 December, at a meeting attended by thirty-two men, Thistlewood was urged to take over the supreme command, as in 1816. He agreed, naming George Edwards his aide-de-camp. A list of available weapons was then drawn up in code : guns, pistols, swords and pikes were referred to as 'speaks', 'tellers', 'thrusts' and 'mows'. Thistlewood made a promise to the meeting − which he failed to keep − to lead them into action within seven days. Edwards then suggested blowing up the House of Commons, but Thistlewood objected on the grounds that innocent people might be killed. Edwards next proposed killing Cabinet Ministers at a fête which the Spanish Ambassador was about to hold, but again Thistlewood refused, this time because there would be ladies present.

According to Edwards, it was agreed in principle that a massacre of Cabinet Ministers was a good idea, as it would make a dramatic beginning to the London rising. At one discussion, said Edwards, Thistlewood remarked that he wished above all to kill Wellington, to which Mrs. Thistlewood replied, 'What, would you not kill Goody?' Goody was apparently her name for Lord Sidmouth.

This, claimed Edwards, inspired Brunt to announce that his friend Tidd particularly wanted to kill Canning, which prompted the butcher Ings to put in his word : 'We must have them before the dissolution of Parliament, or the Buggers will all be gone into the country.'

Thistlewood pointed out that it would be best to wait until the next Grand Cabinet dinner took place, so as to kill the greatest number in one quick coup. 'It will be all anarchy and confusion,' he explained, 'and when the news reaches Carlton House that all the King's Ministers are butchered, the Regent will fly to Brighton and take most of the Horse Guards with him.' In view of what Shegoe had said two years earlier, this seemed to bear out Hobhouse's statement that Thistlewood had despaired of the Metropolis. A massacre of Ministers, Shegoe had written in 1817, 'was not to be attempted if they had numbers sufficient to undertake a more noble and general enterprize, but as the last resort.'

Thistlewood believed that London's workers would support him once his plans had begun to work. He would otherwise be completely wasting his time. But for the attack on the Grand Cabinet, which would be the first objective, he could only count on his immediate circle and Brunt's company of shoemakers. In addition, he hoped it might be possible to recruit some Irishmen, possibly from the colony in Gee's Court, a clutch of hovels and tenements just off Oxford Street. Ever since the Rebellion, Radicals and anarchists had clung to the belief that the sight of Castlereagh's severed head would set off a general insurrection of the Irish in London; therefore, Thistlewood had decided, it might be helpful to carry it through the Irish areas on a pole. Sidmouth's head could accompany it, in order to show the people that the Cabinet had been disposed of.

Obviously the shoemakers and the Irish would stand no chance against units like the Foot Guards and the Household Cavalry. Cannon to stop the horses must be captured; fireballs to burn the barracks must be made. The cannon would need capable gunners to serve them, and Thistlewood was doing his best to recruit some. Sailors in Dockland taverns must have been rather puzzled when a sallow-faced man in a blue greatcoat sidled up and asked them, without any preamble or explanation, how they would like 'to work a big gun'.

As to the Foot Guards, Thistlewood was still hoping that they would defect after three or four hours. He kept sounding them out in taverns, usually in such an oblique manner as to appear even more eccentric than he really was. Once, at the Rose in Wild Street, Holborn, he approached a Guardsman and asked, 'Suppose some night we should begin to kick up a row, would your regiment poke us in the guts?'

'The soldier appeared rather unwilling to enter into conversation,' noted George Edwards.

* * *

The White Lion in Wych Street had lost its licence at the beginning of October, and although Thistlewood continued to hold meetings there from time to time he needed a new headquarters. His choice eventually fell on a public house called the White Hart. Situated on the west side of Brooke's Market, a small square off Gray's Inn Lane, it was very convenient for Brunt and Richard Tidd.

Next door to Tidd, at 4 Hole-in-the-Wall Passage, lived a tall shifty-looking man of forty-five with a lazy eye. This was Robert Adams, once a trooper in the Horse Guards. A shoemaker by trade, he was well known to Brunt, whom he had met when they were both working for the British Army in France. Early in January 1820 Brunt introduced him to Thistlewood, who was interested to learn that Adams had served in the Blues. 'I presume you are a good swordsman?' he asked, to which Adams replied that he could handle a sword well enough to defend himself. Like most of the shoemaking fraternity, Adams lived from hand to mouth, and two days after meeting Thistlewood he was imprisoned for a debt of twenty-three shillings and eightpence.

By this time Thistlewood had decided to rent premises somewhere in the West End of London, the idea being that Ings could run a coffee shop in front as a façade, while bombs and weapons were manufactured in the back. With Brunt and Edwards, Thistlewood spent several days looking for a suitable property, but failed to find one. Then towards the end of the month Brunt reported that there was a vacant upstairs room at 4 Fox Court, for which his landlady, Mary Rogers, wanted three shillings a week. Ings was told to rent it.

Mary Rogers was out when Ings called to see her. When she got back, she learned that her niece had let the empty two-pair-of-stairs back room to a friend of Mr. Brunt. Subsequently Mrs. Rogers told Brunt that she hoped the new lodger was 'a good one.' Brunt replied that he only knew him slightly; he had heard him asking about a room at the nearby public house. However, he supposed that Mr. Ings, who he understood was an out-of-work butcher, would prove satisfactory.

Questioned about it later, Brunt's apprentice Joseph Hale remembered Ings coming to take the empty room. After Ings had 'looked at it, Hale heard Brunt say, 'It will do; go down and give her a shilling.' Hale noticed that Ings gave the key of his room to Brunt whenever he went out. Once Ings left the door ajar, and the inquisitive apprentice saw that there were about twenty long poles in the room, like rough tree branches. Sometimes he heard the sound of sawing and hammering in the room, in which a blue apron belonging to Mrs. Brunt served as a curtain.

Ings evidently had no furniture, because when strangers called chairs had to be taken from Brunt's living-room for them to sit on. One of these strangers was addressed as 'Arthur', or sometimes as 'T'. Strangely, the out-of-work butcher never slept in the room which was costing him three shillings a week, though he paid the rent for a month. Once Mary Rogers saw three men go up the stairs to the room, and one of them was black.

This was William Davidson, the man to whom Williamson had given his pawn ticket. Born in Jamaica, the son of Kingston's Attorney-General, he had been sent to England to study law, but after three years ran away to sea. In 1820 he was thirty-four years old and working as a cabinet-maker. Davidson lived with his wife and six children in Marylebone, at a cottage near Lord's Old Cricket Ground.* His neighbour Robert Wood said that he was a very passionate man, who sometimes got into such a rage that he seemed to be mad. Davidson once told Wood that he had a plate in his head. The locals were polite to his face because they were afraid of him, but behind his back they called him 'the canting mulatto' and said that he was cruel to his wife.

*   *   *

Davidson met Thistlewood through John Harrison, also aged

* Now Dorset Square, Marylebone.

thirty-four, who lived at 6 Little Park Street, Marylebone. After ten years' service in the Life Guards, Harrison had quit the Army in 1814 and was working as a baker. Both he and Davidson were members of the Marylebone Union Reading Society, which had been formed as a result of the Peterloo Massacre. The members paid twopence a week and met every Monday at 54 Queen Street,* Edgware Road, where an elderly teacher named Hazard put a room at their disposal. They read the *Manchester Observer*, which was paid for out of the subscriptions, and talked about parliamentary reform. Harrison attended more often than Davidson, who could not always afford the necessary twopence.

Davidson, like Thistlewood, suspected that Bankes was a spy. At a meeting in January he drew a pistol and threatened to shoot him, whereupon Bankes knocked the pistol aside, produced one of his own, and offered to blow off Davidson's head. At this Davidson burst into laughter, and the two men became friends. Three weeks later Bankes was invited to dine at Davidson's cottage. Thomas Preston was there with three of his four daughters, as well as a sailor named Robert George, who lodged in nearby Lisson Green. Although he did not dine with them, a local tailor named James Wilson kept popping in and out. They drank porter and talked about the King, his Ministers and Parliament. Wilson dropped the remark that 'there would be murdering work yet', which Bankes duly reported to Bow Street.

Meanwhile, in the room at Fox Court, Thistlewood's men had begun to make some of the things they could not afford to buy, including pistol holsters and wrist-slings for sabres and cutlasses. They also made fuses for hand grenades and assembled crude pikes, either by adapting broomsticks or by cutting branches into staves. The pikeheads consisted of old bayonets, or of carpenter's files which were ground to a fine point. The lion's share of the work was done by Edwards, Brunt, Ings and Tidd, though a number of casual helpers were involved at various times. Edwards's list of accomplices contained twenty-seven names, including that of John Williamson, marked 'abroad'.

While the sawing and hammering was going on at Fox Court,

* Now Harrowby Street.

strange things were happening two miles to the west. Children in Marylebone claimed to have seen men stamping about on waste ground carrying sticks on their shoulders, and one day Davidson's neighbour Robert Wood heard 'a sort of thump' as he was working in his garden. Some children came running up to his door and told him that a gentleman had been trying an experiment.

Because they would play such a vital part in his plan, Thistlewood was determined to have his fireballs properly made. He decided to seek advice from Doctor Watson, an expert on explosives and combustibles, who in 1816 had invented a mixture of steel filings, pulverised silver and powdered flint which was so potent that, if a small amount was put into a letter, the recipient blew himself up when he opened the envelope.

*   *   *

On a cold day towards the end of January, Thistlewood and Edwards walked to the big new Debtors' Prison in Whitecross Street, Finsbury: 'dingy and doleful, with its thick door and little wicket, the corridors grated on one side like wild beasts' dens, the wards with their rows of deal tables and benches.'* Watson seemed pleased to see his old colleague again, and explained to him how the fireballs should be made. Junk would have to be picked, rolled into balls, and dipped into a highly inflammable liquid for which Watson supplied the recipe. Once they had been dipped, the fireballs had to be used within twenty-four hours. He also described how to make 'a fire liquid to be contained in a bladder', using hog's lard, rape oil and turpentine.

Presently they talked of the Revolution, and Edwards assured the Doctor that he would soon be at liberty again. Thistlewood mentioned the Proclamation which would be issued when the rising began, and said that he could not decide how to sign it. Watson urged him to use a very common name, such as Robinson. As they left the prison, Thistlewood asked Edwards if he had noticed how jealous the Doctor was; just because Watson's name could not be on the Proclamation, the 'Old Fool' did not want Thistlewood's name on it either.

* *The Graphic,* 15 January 1870.

They walked east along Chiswell Street and called at Caslon's Type Foundry, where Thistlewood had a most useful contact in Harris, the foreman. Chiswell Street ran alongside the Artillery Ground, home of Thistlewood's precious cannon, and Harris was an ex-sailor who knew something about ordnance. When Thistlewood raised the question of ammunition, Harris explained that the H.A.C. cannon were six-pounders, which could be loaded with the tops of railings, broken off with a hammer and tied in a bag. He was definitely going to join in the rising with a party of his friends.

Now that he knew how to make fireballs, Thistlewood was in the market for junk, and asked Harris if he knew where he might get some. As it happened, Harris was keeping his hand on some at the foundry, which he had thought of making into a mat. He hunted it out and gave it to Thistlewood, who tied it up in his handkerchief.

Thistlewood said that he now had sixty men, all armed, and would be needing Harris and his friends in the very near future.

'The sooner the better,' Harris replied.

'We expect it will be Tuesday,' Thistlewood told him. 'There is a Cabinet dinner; we mean to go, and cut all the Ministers' throats. We want a few pikes and such like to be got ready.'

Harris thought that he could probably get about thirty pikes together and a dozen swords.

According to Thistlewood's information, the Cabinet dinner was due to be given by the Earl of Harrowby, Lord President of the Council, whose town house was 39 Grosvenor Square. The area was reconnoitred and a milkwoman pointed out his lordship's residence. William Davidson, who had once worked for Harrowby on his Staffordshire estate, tried to find out more about the dinner, but when some workmen at the house told him that his lordship was out of town, it began to look as if Thistlewood's information was wrong.

Thistlewood detailed several men to shadow Cabinet Ministers, but this was no easy task, since few of the plotters knew them by sight, and the big houses in the West End squares all looked so alike. Abel Hall, a tailor from Finsbury, managed to follow a gentleman's carriage from Westminster to St. James's Square, where Viscount Castlereagh lived. A shoemaker named Potter, a recruit from 'over the water'* did likewise. While these two hung about the square, more carriages arrived, tailed by Edwards, Ings and Brunt. After a quick conference the five of them kept watch on Castlereagh's house, but presently a gentleman riding through the square fell off his horse, and as the servants came out to help him the watchers made themselves scarce.

*   *   *

Released from prison on 30 January, Robert Adams found Thistlewood and his men discussing the implications of the King's death, which had occurred the day before. On the credit side, a lot of Guardsmen from the London barracks had been packed off to Windsor; and even supposing that they could be brought back quickly enough to deal with a rising, Thistlewood said that 'they would be so tired that they could not do anything'. Someone else pointed out that as the soldiers had sworn allegiance to George III, they might not feel obliged to defend George IV. Unfortunately, all the members of the Cabinet had also gone to Windsor, which meant there could be no massacre for the time being.

From 30 January onwards, George Ruthven was assigned exclusively to watching Thistlewood. At the same time Watson's conversations in Whitecross Street were taken down and reported to the Home Office.[13]

In February, Thistlewood and Edwards paid Watson another visit at 'Burdon's Hotel', as the prison was jocularly called. This time Watson took Thistlewood aside and told him not to bring Edwards any more, because he was a dangerous fellow. Thistlewood said that he believed Edwards to be a good man, to which Watson replied, 'Then you differ from many other persons.'

This was undoubtedly true. Soon afterwards Edwards was going up Picket Street when he ran into Samuel Waddington, a printer who was known to the police for his Radical activities. Edwards told Waddington that he was on the lookout for weapons and had plenty of money. There were some swords for

* He lived in Snow's Fields, Southwark.

sale in Clare Market which suited him, said Edwards, but he had already bought some of them, and was afraid it might look odd if he went back for more. Therefore, he suggested, he would give Waddington the money to buy them for him; he was prepared to go up to £300.

Waddington replied that he wanted nothing to do with it. 'I told him that I considered him a most desperate character, where-'upon he drew a dirk out of a walking stick which he carried in his hand, and said in anger, if he thought I would not be among 'them, and that if it was not daylight, he would put it into me.'

Suddenly Edwards's manner changed completely and he asked Waddington where he lived. Waddington wisely refused to tell him.

With William Tunbridge, Edwards tried different tactics. In the presence of Robert Adams and a young carpenter named Richard Bradburn, Edwards delivered his usual tirade against the Government and spoke of 'blowing the bloody buggers' brains out'. Then, producing a brace of pistols, he offered Tunbridge and Bradburn one each. Tunbridge shook his head and said, 'Mr. Edwards, you may tell your employers that they will not catch me in their trap.'

That, at least, is Tunbridge's account of the incident, though whether he and Waddington were telling the truth there is no way of knowing.

Some time later Edwards and Brunt went to see a man named Hetherington, and while they were talking to him Ings and Abel Hall happened to drop in. Hetherington told them that he believed Thistlewood to be a Home Office spy, because someone had recently seen him going into Lord Sidmouth's at eleven o'clock at night. They all laughed at this, and assured Hetherington that it was absurd to think such a thing about Thistlewood. One of them added, jokingly, 'You would have done better to accuse one of us.'

Edwards tried his utmost to discover the names and addresses of Brunt's shoemaking friends, but without much success – though he once accompanied Brunt on what was evidently a sort of inspection tour. To begin with Brunt made two calls in the neighbourhood of Brooke's Market, firstly on a little shoemaker named John Monument at Garden Court, secondly on Richard Tidd. After that he made off to Shoe Lane, but for some reason became very secretive, insisting on going in to see his men alone, while Edwards waited for him outside. 'Brunt turned into Pear Tree or Plum Tree Court,' Edwards reported, 'and said he had two men there. From there Brunt went to another court in Shoe Lane where he said he had a man six feet and a half high; he called him Jack.'

*   *   *

Very little was known for certain about George Edwards; in the House of Commons he was rightly described as 'this man enveloped in mystery'. In 1820 he was aged about thirty-two. According to Edward Aylmer,* his father had lived for some years with a woman in Old Street, Clerkenwell and brought up three children, of whom George was the youngest. The woman was a gin addict. In due course Edwards senior left her and moved to Bristol; being reasonably sure that George was his son, he took him along. Later he sent the boy back to his mother, who was by this time running a 'little-go' or lottery. Apprenticed to Chicani, a statuary who lived near Smithfield, George became a modeller. He turned out figures in plaster of Paris, which he hawked round London and the outskirts, along with recognisable busts of Paine and Carlyle. Aylmer says that he made a very poor living, and often went about barefoot.

Leaving London, he lodged for three years at Windsor and ran a shop in Eton High Street, where his customers included Major-General Sir Herbert Taylor. One of his best-selling lines was a little model of Doctor Keate, the Eton headmaster, which the junior boys bought for target practice.

Alex Richmond believed that Edwards, like Oliver, was recruited to Government service from the Fleet Prison, but Aylmer preferred the theory that he had been introduced to spying by a brother who was 'connected with the police establishment'. This brother, William, was said to have been a Bow Street constable who had done duty at Windsor Castle. One rumour had it that

* Aylmer, op. cit.

The Prince Regent, later George IV.
(Courtesy of The Parker Gallery)

Sir Richard Birnie
*(Guildhall Library,
City of London)*

George Edwards,
from a drawing
published soon after
his disappearance.
*(Guildhall Library,
City of London)*

CONSPIRATORS; or Delegates in Council

Watched by John Bull, senior members of the Government confer with their spies. Seated at the table from left to right are Sidmouth, Thomas Reynolds, John Castle, William Oliver, Canning and Castlereagh. From a print published in July 1817. (*Trustees of the British Museum*)

In this reconstruction of the fight at Cato Street, drawn by Charles Williams, Ellis holds the dying Smithers while Ruthven fires at Thistlewood. Cato Street lies to the left of the picture – the ladder was at the back of the stable. Although he was not present in the loft that night, Thomas Preston is shown (fourth from left). *(Author's collection)*

In George Cruikshank's version of the police raid, Smithers collapses against Ruthven as Ellis fires his pistol. To the left of Thistlewood stand Brunt, grasping sword and pistol, and the bald-headed Tidd. *(Archives Department, Westminster City Library)*

Cato Street, looking north towards John Street, which is just visible through the archway. The stable is on the left, marked A. *(Archives Department, Westminster City Library)*

A back view of the buildings in Cato Street, showing some of Thistlewood's men getting away. *(Trustees of the British Museum)*

John Thomas Brunt

James Ings

William Davidson

Richard Tidd

These portraits of Thistlewood's friends were sketched at the Old Bailey during their trials for high treason.

The house in which Thistlewood was arrested on 24 February 1820. (*Guildhall Library, City of London*)

This photograph, taken shortly before the demolition of Newgate Prison, shows the passage where the remains of Thistlewood, Brunt, Ings, Davidson and Tidd were buried.
To mark the place, the letters T B I D T were cut in the left-hand wall.

Arthur Thistlewood in 1820, 'engraved by Mr. Cooper, from a Drawing taken by Mr. Wivell, in the Sessions House, on the Day Sentence of Death was passed'. *(Archives Department, Westminster City Library)*

Edwards was a compulsive womaniser who needed Blood Money to pay for his debauches. There was also a story that, having drunk too much gin one night at a Radical meeting, he got into a scruffle on his way home, and fired a pistol at a watchman who went to arrest him. Realising that he was in serious trouble, he told the magistrate who examined him that he would disclose some important information if he were let off lightly, and afterwards displayed 'a comparative state of opulence'.

Slightly built and sallow-faced, Edwards was nothing much to look at,[14] but he was a born agent, cool-headed and cunning, with a mind as tidy as his handwriting. His original notes, which are preserved in the Public Record Office,* were written on narrow strips of paper, two or three inches wide and neatly folded into a square. On these strips, some of which are eighteen inches long, he jotted down names, events and conversations as and when he got the chance. The reports which he built up from them were as detailed as any spymaster could wish :

Preston spoke at great length; he adverted to Ancient History, in which he quoted a Persian who overthrew fifteen hundred Thousand Grecians and made them free . . . Ings bought twenty-four poles for pikes. In the evening Bradburn sawed the ends square . . . Harris at the Type Manufactory showed me nine swords that he had been sharpening on the Sunday morning . . . Hartley is endeavouring to go to the Cape of Good Hope in the place of a man that is sick aboard the *Bellellion* – Williamson is Cook to the Passengers on board the same ship . . . Preston occupies one room and a small bedroom adjoining. There are also other rooms on the same floor and the occupiers of one of these can hear what takes place in Preston's room . . . Thistlewood gave Davidson's child a shilling . . .

The notes and the reports do not always tally. The morose Brunt generally used the phrase 'the Ministers' in referring to

* H.O. 42/199.

the Government or the Cabinet, according to the notes; but in the reports this is changed to 'the Buggers'.

In Aylmer's opinion,

> Edwards was not merely an informer, who appeared to accede to the plots of others for the purpose of revealing and defeating them : he was a diabolical wretch who created the treason he disclosed, who went about – a fiend in human form – inflaming distressed and desperate wretches into crimes, in order that he might betray them to justice and make a profit of their blood.

Yet Thistlewood had no need of a George Edwards to push him into treason. As Philip Ziegler has pointed out in his life of Sidmouth,* the Home Secretary knew perfectly well that Thistlewood would hang himself, and his accomplices, provided he were given enough rope. 'The sensible instructions to have given his spy,' Ziegler concludes, 'would have been to hold his peace and let things take their course.'

Edwards did the very opposite; possibly he wanted to hasten a safe retirement. Thistlewood, however, had no suspicion that his thrusting aide-de-camp was a Home Office spy. He did not for a moment doubt that, somewhere in his circle, there was an informer who reported to the hated spymaster at Bow Street, but he was fairly sure that it was Bankes. Bankes had unwittingly become a stalking-horse, and a highly effective one, for John Stafford's number one spy.

* Philip Ziegler, *Addington,* Collins, 1965.

9

'Blood and Wine for Supper!'

EDWARDS was in his element at Fox Court. Dressed in an old flannel jacket he would sit for hours on end, surrounded by gunpowder and musket balls, packing cartridges into tin cases to make grenades. He also picked junk to make fireballs, helped by Thistlewood, Brunt, Ings, Tidd, Harrison and Hall. Ings had been tailing Lord Castlereagh, and considered him a very good-looking fellow : all the same, the butcher declared, he would be damned if he did not kill him before long. This earned him a rebuke from Thistlewood, who said that for Ings to kill Castlereagh on his own would be very improper. All the Ministers must be killed together, because isolated acts did not produce a Revolution, as the shooting of Mr. Perceval had shown.*

The armoury was growing. At Tidd's, which was the main store-place, there were pike shafts, bayonets, stilettoes, ball cartridges and explosives, including a very large grenade made from an old coffee roaster. Firearms, however, were still very scarce, despite the boast of a friendly pigeon fancier named Sturges that he could get them a thousand stand of arms at an hour's notice. Harrison thought they should make a raid on a bishop's house in Cavendish Square, where he said there were a great many firearms; they were kept in the hall, and could be seen from the street. He thought the house might be the Bishop of Durham's, and in this he was correct. The Bishop lived at 16 Cavendish Square, but the firearms in his hall consisted of one loaded blunderbuss and two loaded pistols, which were kept on hooks over the fireplace.

When he was not working at Fox Court, Edwards spent a

* The Prime Minister who was assassinated in 1812.

good deal of his time trying to involve backsliders like George Pickard in Thistlewood's plot. Thomas Chambers received several visits, but when Edwards told him that he must be ready to fight against the tyrants, Chambers replied that he had nothing to fight with. In that case, said Edwards, a weapon would be supplied.

The next time they met, Chambers tried to pretend that he had no idea what Edwards was talking about. 'You are not such a fool,' Edwards retorted. 'We mean to destroy Ministers.' Seeing that Chambers would not commit himself, Edwards clapped his hand against the wall of the room and warned him, 'This is all lath and plaster, and you shan't be safe; we'll blow you out of your bed.'

On 8 February Edwards and Brunt met an Irishman named Burke as they were walking up the Haymarket, and stopped to talk to him. Burke was a shoemaker, well acquainted with Brunt, and a member of the Marylebone Union. They exchanged a few items of Radical gossip, and Burke said that he was forming a select party of Irish for a bit of action; but when Brunt and Edwards showed interest, he added quickly that his party would not join in any English enterprise until the last moment, for fear the English would betray them.

The English were waiting only for the next Cabinet dinner, but of this there was no sign. Every morning Thistlewood went to Peele's Coffee House in Fetter Lane, where the best selection of town and country newspapers in London was kept, and looked for details of forthcoming functions. Eventually the task of reading so many columns of print defeated him, so he shared it with Edwards. While his aide-de-camp scoured the *New Times,* Thistlewood checked the *Morning Post.*

According to Henry Hobhouse's diary, in January it had been agreed to hold a Cabinet dinner on 9 February, but it was postponed to the twenty-third because of the King's death.

On the eighteenth Thistlewood went to see Harris at the Type Foundry to talk about artillery. For some time past the tops of cast-iron railings had been disappearing in Holborn and Finsbury, and Harris had about a hundredweight ready to be made up into bags for cannon-shot. Thistlewood told him that, as he had been on board ship and understood the use of 'Great Guns', he had better attach himself to Cooke, who was responsible for capturing the cannon and getting them to the Mansion House.

Harris agreed, and reported that the guns at the adjoining Artillery Ground were in good working order; the H.A.C. had been out firing with them on the day of the King's funeral. This was reassuring in more ways than one, for during the last four months of Despard's plot, as Thistlewood believed, the Government had ordered the hammers to be removed from the muskets in the Bank of England vaults, knowing that Despard meant to use them.

By now, according to Robert Adams, Thistlewood's men were saying that they must either act soon or go to work, as 'they were all so poor, they could not wait any longer'. Thistlewood, says Edwards, even considered abandoning the massacre idea and attacking the Bank of England, which he thought might have an even greater moral effect than killing Ministers. But he did not think that his men could be persuaded to do it; and in any case Brunt, whose influence seemed to be very great now, preferred the massacre.

Edwards himself continued to radiate confidence, and meeting George Pickard on the nineteenth told him, 'You bugger, Pickard, you must fight before long.'

*   *   *

The following day was Sunday, and more men gathered in the butcher's room at Fox Court than Brunt's apprentice had ever seen there before. They included Thistlewood, Brunt, Ings, Davidson, Edwards, Harrison and Hall. William Cooke, the man who would direct the cannon party, was also present; so were James Wilson, the Marylebone tailor, Richard Bradburn, the good-looking young carpenter, and a morose man from Southwark named John Palin, who was a child's chair maker. Robert Adams arrived at eleven o'clock.

There had been a heavy fall of snow that morning, and the sky was overcast. The room was so dark that when someone spoke to Adams, it was a moment or so before he realised that it was his next-door neighbour, Richard Tidd.

'Gentlemen,' said Arthur Thistlewood, 'I presume you all know what we are met for.' Pausing for a moment, and glancing at the door as if afraid of being overheard, he added, 'The West End Job.' He then began to outline his plan.

He himself would lead the West End Job, as he called the Cabinet Massacre, which would require forty or fifty men. Meanwhile Cooke's party, supported by an Irish contingent from Gee's Court, would seize the cannon at Gray's Inn Lane and Bunhill Row and load them with powder. Some of Cooke's men would carry sledge-hammers, in case they needed to break off more paling-tops for shot.

Harrison, the former Life Guards trooper, would set fire to the Horse Barracks in King Street, helped by James Wilson. Palin had a roving commission, and might fire virtually whatever buildings he pleased, though his primary target was the barracks in Albany Street.

If the West End Job went according to plan, Thistlewood's force would move back east towards Holborn and the City, gathering up Cooke's party on the way, and summon the Mansion House. Three cannon would be posted next to Royal 'Change and three more at Cornhill, and if the first summons was not obeyed they would open fire. It was assumed that the Mansion House would then surrender. If any hitch occurred in the early stages, Thistlewood and Cooke would send messengers to Saint Sepulchre's Church to exchange reports.

Should there be a Cabinet dinner before the following Wednesday, 23 February, so much the better. If not, the idea of wiping out the Cabinet in one swift raid must be dropped; Ministers would have to be killed as and where they could be found.

Thistlewood's outline seemed to satisfy everyone except Palin. An ex-seaman who had also been a corporal in the East London Militia, he wanted to know where the men were coming from. 'You talk of taking from forty to fifty men for the West End Job,' he said. 'I should like to know, then, where you are to find the men to take the cannon in Gray's Inn Lane and the Artillery Ground, for *I* can't say where they are to be got, although you may know more on the subject than I do. I want to know also, in calling upon the men I intend to go to, if I can tell them in fact what is to be done.'

It was generally agreed that what Palin told his men was entirely up to him, but his question about the men who would capture the guns was not answered. Thistlewood merely observed that on Tuesday or Wednesday they must get together what men they could and give them a treat.

'Damn my eyes,' Adams heard Brunt say, 'I have not done little or no work for some time, but I have got a pound note for that purpose, and I will be damned if I do not spend it upon the men we have got.'

'Where can we take them to?' asked Thistlewood. 'I should suppose we might have the room below stairs at the White Hart.'

'I do not know,' Brunt replied. 'I do not much like to go there after what has been said, but never mind. I do not see that we have no cause, as time gets on, to be afraid of the bloody Traps; for if they come into the room they shall not get out again.'

He was talking about a rumour that the police were watching the White Hart. Later that day, according to Adams, the landlord said that he had been questioned by two police officers, one from Bow Street and the other from Hatton Garden, about Radical meetings being held on his premises.

* * *

The next day being Monday, the Marylebone Union was due to meet at Hazard's schoolroom off the Edgware Road. Through the good offices of Harrison and Davidson, who belonged to both groups, the Union had given Thistlewood's party a modest amount of gunpowder, and also contributed a shilling or two now and then. As a result of their talk with Burke in the Haymarket, Brunt and Edwards had attended the Union meeting on the fourteenth, and had suggested a merger between the Union and the powerful forces being assembled by Thistlewood. Feeling that the leader's authority was needed to clinch the matter, on the evening of the twenty-first Thistlewood went to Queen Street with George Edwards.

Without going into details, he told the Marylebone men that something important was going to happen on the following Wednesday, and asked if any members of the Union would support him; he was expecting to find fifty good men amongst them. This was absurdly optimistic, since the average turn-out at the schoolroom was ten or twelve members, of whom three were involved with Thistlewood already. A typical meeting might consist of Hazard, who was over seventy, Greener the secretary, a footman named Simmons, a cowman named Firth, James Wilson, Davidson, Harrison and Burke. Occasionally a labourer named Emanuel Francis joined them. He was not a paying member, but being unable to keep proper accounts of his work he went to Hazard for evening lessons, and as his lesson ended at eight o'clock, by which time the Union business was just beginning, he stayed behind once or twice to listen to what went on.

On the twenty-first, according to Francis, eight or perhaps ten members turned up; none of them showed much interest in what Thistlewood had to say, though Greener told him that 'he dared say there would be plenty to act'. Thistlewood declared that there would never be 'a better time to stir in England', as there was an insurrection going on in Spain and a Prince had just been murdered in France.

His audience was still not impressed. Only a week ago Brunt and Edwards had been boasting about the strength of their organisation; now here was the leader openly admitting that he was unable to act for the want of fifty men. Supplying a powerful movement with a few shillings and the odd bag of powder was one thing, but abetting a handful of mumpers in a forlorn hope was definitely something else. 'This is a very different story from what I have been told before,' said John Firth. 'It was then said that you had plenty of men.'

Thistlewood tried to explain that he did not need the Union members for his main object, but for 'other things to be done at the same moment'. Edwards recorded that 'a considerable altercation then took place, and much doubt was expressed whether we should be able to succeed'.

As they came away, Thistlewood told him, 'You see, the Marylebone Union are not so forward as we expected.' The outcome of his visit, so different from what he had anticipated, thoroughly depressed him, and he even began to talk of failure. If the murder of Ministers did not lead to a Revolution, he said, they must attack either Child's or Coutts' Bank, and take enough money to get them out of the country. 'If we have a man wounded who cannot live', he added gloomily, 'his head must be cut off and carried away with us.' John Stafford's house must be entered and searched, as no doubt a list of all the spies in Government pay would be found there.

Next day, 22 February, the *New Times* announced that a Grand Cabinet dinner would be held the following evening at Lord Harrowby's in Grosvenor Square. This was a minor scoop for the paper, which was run by Doctor John Stoddart, a former leader writer on *The Times* who was popularly known as Doctor Slop; no other paper carried the item.

When Edwards arrived at Fox Court he asked Thistlewood if he had seen anything about a Cabinet dinner. Thistlewood said no, there was nothing in the *Morning Post,* which he had checked as usual. Explaining that he had stopped to look at the *New Times* window in Fleet Street, where the latest edition of the paper was displayed, Edwards broke the news. Thistlewood immediately sent someone to buy a copy, and Brunt said Damn his eyes, he now believed there was a God, since the Buggers had been called together; it was what he had long prayed for.

The paper duly arrived, and the announcement was found in the 'Fashionable Mirror' on page three : 'The Earl of Harrowby gives a Grand Cabinet Dinner to-morrow at his house in Grosvenor Square.' Thistlewood, reported Edwards, 'read the advertisement very loud, which immediately inspired the whole room with hilarity.' Then, saying that things must be arranged at once, he began to go over in his mind the forty men who would be needed. Bradburn could bring nine men, and Brunt about eleven, which with Thistlewood himself made twenty-three. Then

there were Ings and Abel Hall, Tidd, Harrison, Wilson, Davidson and two men called Overy – grand total thirty-one. The
remainder, said Thistlewood, would have to come from the
Marylebone Union.

After all the months of planning and frustration, the situation
seemed almost too good to be true. Apart from creating a power
vacuum, the Cabinet massacre was bound to have a tremendous
moral effect as the news spread that the Ministers had been
butchered, the King had fled, a Provisional Government was
sitting at the Mansion House, a Committee of Public Safety was
being formed . . .

What Guardsman or trooper, what magistrate even, would
dare to act against him then? Within a few hours he would be
master of London; but for the present there was a lot of work to
be done and not much time. Premises at the West End of town
must be found, so that the weapons could be moved nearer to
Grosvenor Square, which was over two miles away from the Fox
Court headquarters and Tidd's armoury. Lord Harrowby's house
had to be watched, to see if there were police officers stationed
there, or any other signs of a trap.

Number thirty-nine was on the south side of Grosvenor Square.
Thistlewood planned to knock at the door, carrying either a letter
or something which looked like a red dispatch box. When a
servant opened the door, Thistlewood would tell him to take the
letter or box to the Ministers at once, while he waited in the
hall with one of his men. As soon as the servant had turned his
back, the street door would be opened to admit the rest of the
gang. If the servants tried to interfere in any way, grenades
would be thrown into their quarters and other parts of the house.

According to Adams, Ings volunteered to enter the dining-
room first, armed with a pair of pistols, a cutlass, a butcher's
knife and two large bags. 'Well, my lords,' he would announce to
the astonished Ministers, 'I have got as good men here as the
Manchester Yeomanry. Enter, citizens, and do your duty!'

The others would then rush in and fall to work with pikes
and pistols, 'murdering as fast as they could'. None would be
spared; if there were any good men present at the dinner they

would be killed for keeping bad company.

Thistlewood wanted two good swordsmen to lead in the killing party, and chose Harrison and Adams, both ex-troopers of the Household Cavalry. Harrison, who had often talked about crowning the Prince Regent with an axe, was rather a simple-minded man : he said that he would swear after the massacre that the Duke of Wellington turned out to be the biggest coward in the room, and begged for mercy on his knees. This would be 'very degrading' to the Duke's relatives.

Thistlewood decided that Harrison had 'better take the stair-case', and that the two swordsmen should be Adams and David-son. When all the victims were dead, Ings would cut off the heads of Sidmouth and Castlereagh and bring them away in his two bags, so that they could be carried on poles along Oxford Street and Holborn. 'Well,' Robert Adams is supposed to have said (though he always denied it), 'we are going to kill His Majesty's Ministers, and will have blood and wine for supper!'

*　　*　　*

In the two-pair-of-stairs back room at Fox Court, which reeked of newly-dipped fireballs, men whom Adams had never seen before were flinting pistols, and Thistlewood was in unusually good spirits. 'Well, my lads, this looks like something,' he said approvingly. 'This looks as if something is going to be done.'

With the rising due to start in less than twenty-four hours, something had to be done about the Proclamation. This had always been a problem, because the only printers who would touch such a document were closely watched by the police (hence Doctor Watson's advice to sign it 'Robinson'.) In January Thistle-wood had given the print order to a man at Smithfield named Davison, who had turned out Radical bills often enough in the past. Although he kept the hand-written copy for several weeks, Davison never attempted to supply the order, of which he later denied all knowledge.

At least six copies of the Proclamation would have to be posted up near the buildings fired by Palin, otherwise the people who came out to watch would not understand what was happening. Consequently there was nothing for it but to write them out by hand, and in the eleventh-hour rush of 22 February the original text was drastically reduced. Of these manuscript Proclamations, all that Adams could remember afterwards was:

Your tyrants are destroyed, the Friends of Liberty are called upon to come forward, as the Provisional Government is now sitting. –
           J. Ings Secretary February 23rd 1820

It seems unlikely that even the shortened version was quite so brief as this, and Adams himself said that he thought some words which he could not recall might have been added above the signature. George Edwards could quote a version which ran to 199 words.

Thistlewood wrote out two or three copies himself, but his hand shook so much that he had to stop; according to Abel Hall, he was trembling because 'the numbers had not come that he expected'. When Brunt arrived, claims Hall, he was surprised to find so few men present, but said that his own men would no doubt come at any minute.

Edwards had been detailed to cover the servants' hall at Grosvenor Square, for which task he said he needed a blunderbuss. The only one available was John Williamson's, which was still in pledge for seven shillings at the pawnshop in Berwick Street, and for which Davidson was holding the ticket. Seven shillings was too large a sum for Thistlewood to find, but he remembered that he had four prints at his lodgings which could be turned into cash – three of the Storming of Seringapatam and one of Sir Francis Burdett. He fetched them from Stanhope Street and gave them to Edwards, who claimed that he sold one of them to his brother for two shillings, and the other three to a dealer in Old Compton Street for five shillings and sixpence.

This dealer was a carver and gilder named Thomas Jennings, who later denied that he paid Edwards anything like five-and-six; when Edwards asked twelve shillings for the prints, Jennings told him they were practically worthless and offered sixpence, which Edwards accepted. Nonetheless, Edwards succeeded in getting the seven shillings from some source or other, and Davidson redeemed the blunderbuss next day.

Edwards also found time on the twenty-second to visit Thomas Chambers, and asked if he might leave a bag in his care. When Chambers asked what was in it Edwards replied, 'Oh, only a few pistols and such like.' Chambers refused to have anything to do with 'such a Despard's business', so Edwards went away, saying that all such cowards should be blown out of their beds. At about the same time William Davidson took half a dozen files to a Marylebone locksmith named James Pocock and told him to point them. When Pocock asked if they were for turning tools, Davidson replied, 'No, they are for turning Men's Guts!'

All over the city, from Gray's Inn Lane to Edgware Road, events and conversations were taking place which would lead men like Pocock to the witness stand at the Old Bailey, and other residents of Marylebone to even stranger places : two of them to a stinking prison hulk, and one more to a scaffold outside Newgate Prison.

*　　*　　*

For reasons not recorded, Emanuel Francis had decided not to have any more evening lessons at Hazard's schoolroom. When he went along to Queen Street to break the news to Hazard, he found him musing over a strange conversation which he had had with John Firth, the cowman. This man had urged Hazard not to miss seeing a bonfire which someone would be lighting the following night, and Hazard had promised that he would hobble out as best he could; but he was not very good on his feet, being paralytic. Francis asked Hazard what Firth was talking about, but Hazard did not really know. He said Firth had told him that they meant to set a house on fire, and that would draw a great many people together, and then they would put themselves in possession of pikes or guns, and the Life Guards would not be able to stand against them, and they would drive all before them.

That evening, says Robert Adams, Thistlewood swore that he would leave Stanhope Street at nine o'clock next morning, and never go up his stairs again without either a gold chain round his neck or a wooden leg. He had promised himself thirty years of comfort, he added, to make up for the hardships he had suffered in the past.

Earlier in the day a very curious incident had taken place, involving Lord Harrowby and Thomas Hiden, a former cow-keeper turned dairyman. Hiden lived at Manchester Mews, Marylebone, and was acquainted with James Wilson, the tailor. One day in February, if Hiden's story is true (he could not recall the exact date), Wilson came up to him in the street and asked him to join a party which meant to 'destroy His Majesty's Ministers' as they sat at dinner. On the twenty-second, according to the official Government version, Hiden approached Lord Harrowby as he was riding in Hyde Park and warned him to cancel the Cabinet dinner arranged for the following night, as otherwise he and his colleagues would be murdered. He also gave Harrowby a letter for Lord Castlereagh, whom Hiden had been trying to contact.

'The plan is laid to take your lives,' this letter began. 'When the Cabbinett Council is at Dinner these Villings ar Gooin to Enter in to the House with great things they Heve made of Gunpowder.' The writer warned 'your biggest inemy is Thissell-wood', and recommended a search of Gee's Court, Oxford Street.

The following day Lord Harrowby had a further talk with Hiden in the Park, this time 'among the young plantations in the Ring'. Hiden also had another discussion with Wilson, who told him that all the Irish in Gee's Court were 'in it', but refused to act until the English had actually begun, having been deceived by them so often in the past.

To Thistlewood, the news that all the Gee's Court Irish were 'in it' would have been very welcome. He envisaged using forty men to do the West End Job and another hundred to capture the cannon at Gray's Inn Lane and Bunhill Row, but these 140 men existed only in his imagination. According to the list compiled by George Edwards, the conspiracy consisted of Thistle-wood and twenty-seven others. If we add Edwards, whom Thistlewood naturally included in all his calculations, the total becomes twenty-eight. There was also a mysterious tall man who joined the plot very late in February. Adams did not know who he was and the other plotters, though unperturbed by his presence, never addressed him by name. Perhaps, like Adams, they concluded that since he was there, someone must have vouched for him.

Edwards did not list Charles Cooper or John Monument, who were both Brunt's men. He also omitted Harris of the Type Foundry, his young nephew, and a friend of Harris's named Murray. With the tall stranger, they make a grand total of thirty-four. Nine of the men on Edwards's list, however, took no part in the 1820 plot, though some of them were admittedly 'Old Jacks'* and former Spenceans. According to Bankes they felt, like Watson, that 'the time for resorting to arms had not arrived'. Edwards also listed Bankes himself, who was a spy; Walker, who was in Manchester; John Williamson, who was somewhere on the high seas; and Doctor Watson, who was in prison for debt. Two more, William Tunbridge and Thomas Chambers, refused point blank to help.

The order of battle thus shrinks to nineteen men, not all of whom would be available for the West End Job. Cooke would be leading the artillery squad, assisted by Harris, while Palin would be roving with his fireballs over Holborn. Preston was lame and unreliable.† In other words, Thistlewood had only fifteen men for the massacre, a discrepancy of twenty-five, and in the likely event of the Gee's Court Irish failing to appear, the total force available for seizing six pieces of cannon and man-handling them to the Mansion House would comprise Harris, Preston and Cooke.

The man whom Thistlewood expected to lead the low Irish detachment was a bricklayer named Thomas Dwyer. Dwyer was something of a mystery to his friends, because he was hardly ever seen to lay any bricks, though he sometimes attended an establishment called The Mill, where Marylebone's paupers were allowed to work for an hour or so a day. It was through meeting

* Jacobins.
† Harrison and Wilson were to take part in the massacre first and set fire to the Horse Barracks afterwards.

William Davidson at The Mill that Dwyer had been introduced to Thistlewood, who took him to a public house in Molyneux Street at the beginning of February. On that occasion Thistlewood told Dwyer that he had been in five or six revolutions, and that Ireland was in a disturbed state.

On 23 February Dwyer was taken by Harrison to Fox Court, where he found Thistlewood, Brunt, Davidson and a few others. Grenades and powder were being put into a bag, to be taken to Marylebone along with some pikes. Thistlewood asked Dwyer how many Irish he could muster.

'Twenty-six or seven,' Dwyer replied.

Thistlewood told him to be at the Pomfret Castle in Wigmore Street at six o'clock that evening. According to Dwyer: 'We were then to go to the Foundling Hospital, to knock at the porter's lodge, to put a pistol to the porter's breast, and then to turn round to the right hand, where I would see five- or six-and-twenty stand of arms.'

At this stage the Home Office was doing everything possible to disguise the fact that George Edwards was a spy, so the appearance of Hiden the dairyman was most opportune. So was Thistlewood's talk with Dwyer who, as Henry Hobhouse wrote in his diary, had been 'seduced to promise aid to the conspirators'. Returning home about noon, Dwyer went to tell a Major James what he had seen and heard at Fox Court, and was taken to the Home Office. According to Hobhouse, Dwyer arrived at the Office 'in great agitation' at about three o'clock. He reported that Thistlewood's gang would assemble for the massacre at a public house called the Horse and Groom. This was in John Street, Marylebone,* a turning off the right hand side of the Edgware Road, about half a mile north of Tyburn turnpike.

*   *   *

If the official Government version of events is true, the announcement of a Grand Cabinet dinner in the *New Times* was quite genuine. Even after Hiden had warned of the impending massacre, the Duke of Wellington suggested that the Cabinet

---

* Now Crawford Place.

should still assemble at Lord Harrowby's house, which could be filled with soldiers dressed as servants, so as to make sure of catching Thistlewood red-handed. His colleagues decided that it would be too dangerous. It was agreed, however, that nothing should be said to the servants, though pistols were issued out to them, and Lord Harrowby's French chef went on preparing his special dishes.* Now that they knew of the plot, wrote Hobhouse in his diary, Cabinet Ministers realised that for some time past, especially when leaving their carriages at night, they had had the feeling that someone was watching them from the shadows.

So much for the official version. As to what really happened, the facts speak for themselves.

By 18 February Thistlewood's plot had started to collapse for want of money, and he knew that unless he acted without much more delay he would lose most of his men. This was why, at the meeting on 20 February, he announced the deadline for the West End Job as the following Wednesday. Unless there was a Cabinet dinner on that day, he declared, then the Ministers would be killed wherever they could be found.

In other words, a dozen armed assassins would have vanished into London, and no member of the Cabinet would have been safe in his own house, let alone on the streets of the city. Two days later, news that a Cabinet dinner would take place on 23 February (the same date as Thistlewood's deadline) appeared exclusively in a newspaper subsidised by the Government. Thistlewood's original plan of a massacre under one roof now became workable again, and was re-adopted. Thus once more George Edwards knew exactly when and where the assassins meant to strike; once more the Home Office and John Stafford were in control. That same day, the man at whose house the massacre would take place was warned by Hiden, who had been invited *in the street* to join the conspiracy. The day afterwards, the gang's rendezvous was disclosed by Dwyer, enabling the police to plan Thistlewood's capture without betraying the fact that Edwards was a spy.

---

* It was said that, when he finally learned that the dinner was cancelled, he threw them on the fire.

Edwards was up with the lark on the twenty-third. At Fox Court he picked up Williamson's blunderbuss and loaded it with three musket balls. Someone gave him a rope ladder, so that he could climb over the area railings at Lord Harrowby's if the gate which led to the servants' quarters should be locked. He was due to take the four o'clock watch in Grosvenor Square.

Meanwhile the others would be making their way by twos and threes to the Edgware Road, carrying the arms and explosives. Everything was being taken except the ball cartridges from Tidd's and the paling-tops from the Type Foundry. Davidson had said that he could get all the cartridges they needed in Marylebone, and there was no point in moving the paling-tops from Caslon's, where they were handy to the H.A.C. cannon.

For security reasons the plotters would make only a brief appearance at the Horse and Groom in John Street, where Davidson, Harrison and Wilson would be keeping a lookout for them. From the public house they would be taken to another place, which for the present was a closely guarded secret.

At Bow Street, police orders for the night's operation had been issued by John Stafford, the man whose raid had smashed Despard's gang in 1802. Then, as now, the rendezvous had been an obscure public house in a working-class district.

On that memorable night eighteen years before, Stafford's force had consisted entirely of police Patroles drawn from London, Kent and Surrey. As the Government knew, however, there was one important difference between Despard and Thistlewood, insofar as springing the trap was concerned. Unlike Despard, who did most of his plotting in taverns, Thistlewood had several private places at his disposal, including two armouries in Holborn and one in Finsbury, where pikes and other weapons could be kept. To spring the trap on Thistlewood, therefore, the police alone were not enough; because Stafford and his understrappers, though quite accustomed to facing the rather unreliable hand-guns of the day, were hardly equipped to do battle with men wielding home-made pikes. That called for muskets and bayonets . . .

The trap was now almost set and a warrant for Thistlewood and thirteen others was sworn by Henry Hobhouse. Clearly this document could not have been drawn up solely on the information supplied by Hiden and Dwyer, since it named Brunt, Ings, Tidd, Davidson, Edwards, Adams, Palin, Potter, Hall, Harrison, Wilson, Cooke and Strange. Except for Strange and Edwards, all these names were on the list compiled by Edwards for the Home Office.

The warrant was delivered to Mr. Birnie at Bow Street at about seven o'clock.

10

The Battle of Cato Street

FEW BUILDINGS in Marylebone were more than seventy years
old. In the 1760s the district had been mostly hayfields and
sandpits, and travellers going north would stop and check over
their pistols when they reached the White Hart, which stood in
what was then known as Wig More Row.* By 1820 most of the
ground between Oxford Street and the New Road (as Marylebone Road was called) had been developed, with buildings and
thoroughfares which all reflected the Georgian liking for sym-
metry and straight lines. There were few of the narrow courts
and winding alleys which filled older parts of London, though
Marylebone Lane, once a country footpath running along the
Tyburn's eastern bank, still went its own crooked way.

The Tyburn had given its name to many things in Marylebone, such as the gates and turnpike at the western end of Oxford
Street, and the famous gallows which for six centuries operated
nearby. Most Marylebone people over fifty had vivid memories
of the Tyburn hangings, with crowds laughing and cheering
round the scaffold, and mothers holding up their infants to clasp
hands with the swinging corpses, convinced that the touch of
Dead Man's Sweat cured almost anything from wens to scrofula.

From Tyburn Gate the turnpike ran north to Edgware and
formed Marylebone's western boundary. This Edgware Road
was a very ancient thoroughfare, having been an important highway under the Roman occupation, and a track long before that.
Going towards Edgware, the sixth turning on the right from
Tyburn turnpike was Queen Street, where the Marylebone
Union held their weekly meetings, and the next turning after

* Now Wigmore Street.

that was John Street. These two sidestreets were connected by three smaller ones running north and south, of which the middle one was Cato Street.

In effect Cato Street was an oblong court, surrounded by buildings on all four sides, and entered by square archways from John Street and Queen Street. These archways were like miniature tunnels. At the John Street end, vehicles could pass into Cato Street by a narrow carriageway, but the 'tunnel' at the Queen Street end was closed by posts. The residents of this odd, fag-end of a place belonged to what Regency newspapers called 'a humble sphere of life'.

On the left hand side of the street at the top end was a small, square, two-storey building. Owned by a General Watson, it had once been used for stabling his horses. There were still three stalls in the ground-floor stable, part of which was screened off to form a small carriage- or cart-house. From the ground floor, opposite the door, a narrow and almost perpendicular ladder led from the stable up to the hayloft. At the side of this loft there were two smaller rooms, which were formed by a partition.

General Watson was abroad, and the building was rented by John Firth, a former servant of the general's, and the man who had spoken to Hazard about the bonfire. Firth had recently been housing his cows in the ground-floor stable, but round about Christmas time he had taken a shed nearer his home, so the little building in Cato Street was unoccupied. It was not quite empty, though. In the hayloft was a bench, left by a carpenter who had once rented the top floor, and some tools; in the ground-floor cart-house an old cabriolet was slowly falling apart.

On 22 February, according to Firth, John Harrison said that he would like to rent the stable so that he might keep a horse and cart there. Firth had known Harrison since the Peace, a matter of five years or more, and since they were both members of the Marylebone Union, they often met at Mr. Hazard's in Queen Street on a Monday night. In February 1820, as Firth well knew, Harrison did not own a horse, but he claimed that his brother was going to buy one for him. Firth agreed to rent him the stable on a six week tenancy at five shillings a week.

Almost opposite the stable, at the corner of Cato Street and John Street, stood the Horse and Groom public house; and from two o'clock in the afternoon of 23 February, a man who looked very like George Ruthven sat drinking in the tap.

*   *   *

It was certainly an exciting day for the people of Cato Street. At three o'clock Elizabeth Weston, who lived at number one, saw a man enter the stable carrying a large bag on his back. At number forty-five, almost opposite, lived nine-year-old Jane Isaacs; she saw a man go into the building between four and five o'clock, balancing on his shoulder what looked like a bundle of poles wrapped in sacking. At six o'clock Mrs. Weston saw a man of colour standing outside the stable. Minutes later he knocked at her door and asked her to light a candle which he was holding. She thought his manner rather impudent.

Richard Munday at number three also saw this man of colour. Munday knew Firth well, because though a gardener by trade he was also a spare-time vet, and bled Firth's cows from time to time. That afternoon he saw that men were nailing up sacking inside the windows of Firth's stable, as though to stop anyone looking in. He decided to keep an eye on things.

The black man had a companion, later proved to be Harrison. While Munday was watching these two men, the coat of one of them came open, revealing that he was wearing a number of belts – two round his shoulders (one each way) and two more round his waist. Two pistols were stuck into one of these belts, and as the man stooped down something stuck out on his right hand side.

George Ruthven was not sitting in the Horse and Groom by chance, although, according to Henry Hobhouse, Dwyer and his story about the Horse and Groom did not reach the Home Office until three o'clock. In fact, it was becoming increasingly difficult to maintain the fiction that it was Hiden and Dwyer, not George Edwards, who had given Thistlewood's plot away. Ruthven subsequently gave five separate and slightly different accounts of his movements on the twenty-third.*

* One at an inquest and four at the Old Bailey.

It seems that he first arrived in Cato Street at about two o'clock, one hour before Dwyer reached the Home Office. After spending several hours on watch he left in the late afternoon, returning at about six. Officially, Bow Street knew nothing of what was afoot until after seven, when it was announced that a number of officers, constables and Patroles would be wanted for special duty that night. However, Ruthven had already taken one officer to Cato Street that afternoon, and when he went back in the evening he took several more. By half past six the stable was being watched by Patroles Robert Chapman and William Lee. They saw four men enter the building: Davidson, Harrison, a bootmaker named Charles Cooper, and James Gilchrist, an out-of-work shoemaker.

After standing for some time at the John Street corner, Chapman and Lee decided that they were becoming too conspicuous, and moved into adjacent Molyneux Street. Soon after they got there, says Chapman, Thistlewood approached, 'and as it were got between us, and looked us thoroughly in the face, and we did the same to him. Lee observed it was very rude, and I said perhaps the gentleman thought he knew us, and the man muttered "It's a mistake", and turned upon his heel and went back to Cato Street.'

Thistlewood was probably looking for Tidd, whose failure to arrive at the stable on time had raised all sorts of grim possibilities. Perhaps he had been arrested, or perhaps he had decided to withdraw at the last minute. Worst of all, he might even be an informer who had betrayed the West End Job to the Traps.

In fact, at 6.30 Tidd was only just setting out from Hole-in-the-Wall Passage with John Monument, the little shoemaker who lived in nearby Garden Court, and who had been brought into the plot by Brunt.

'Where are we going?' Monument asked. 'The House of Commons?'

Tidd said No, there were too many soldiers about that place; they were going to a Cabinet dinner in Grosvenor Square.

*   *   *

Lord Sidmouth had ordered the trap to be closed by a party of the Second Foot Guards, whose barracks in Portman Square were less than half a mile from the Horse and Groom. Only a few police officers would be needed, mainly to serve the warrant. For Mr. Richard Birnie this was bad news.

Whether Birnie had been hoping to command a strong combined force of Runners and Patroles, as Stafford had done in 1802, is not known for sure. What is certain is that Sir Nathaniel Conant was about to retire, and that Birnie was as determined as ever to succeed him. He knew that his own brusque manners had earned him many influential enemies, and that Baker of Marlborough Street was generally thought to be next in line; but he evidently felt that if he could score a great personal success in capturing Thistlewood, things would look very different. Lord Sidmouth's arrangements seemed to have frustrated him, since the lion's share of the action and any resulting glory would belong to the Foot Guards.

As Cato Street lay in the area administered by Marlborough Street Public Office, the warrant was signed by Robert Baker. As we have seen, it was delivered to Birnie at seven o'clock and named only thirteen accomplices, whereas the previous day Thistlewood had spoken of a task force of thirty-one, not counting the men of the Marylebone Union. It is not known whether Birnie had been expecting a warrant for thirty-odd men, but subsequent events tend to suggest this. Afterwards, in explaining why the policemen who went to Cato Street arrived piecemeal, he wrote, 'Those who came late were not apprized till late, I had left orders at the Office to send them as soon as they could be collected.'

What was it that caused this last minute confusion, so untypical of Bow Street's methods? Is it possible that when Birnie examined the warrant, and found that it named only fourteen men, he decided that he need not play second fiddle to some young Guards officer after all? Describing the part which the police played that night, Percy Fitzgerald, the Bow Street historian, wrote : *

* Percy H. Fitzgerald, *Chronicles of Bow Street Police Office,* 1888.

They were to have been supported by a body of Foot Guards, but unluckily these were not ready at the time, and the police proceeded without them. It was said later that this was owing to some jealousy on the part of the force, who purposely started earlier.

In view of his unrivalled experience of police raids, one would have expected John Stafford to be in at the kill that night, but at the last minute he was summoned to the Home Office. Birnie himself left for John Street, stopping en route at Portman Barracks to give the Guards their instructions.

By 6.30 Ruthven, Wright, Chapman and Lee were already in the Cato Street area. The next batch of police to arrive consisted of Westcott, Nixon, Townsend, Champion and Brooks, bringing the force at Birnie's disposal to nine.* At half past seven Stafford dispatched four more from Bow Street by coach – James Ellis, Benjamin Gill, John Surman and Richard Smithers. Smithers, formerly attached to Queen Square Police Office, was rather stout, and though much younger than John Stafford resembled him in looks and build.

At John Street these four were greeted by Birnie, who asked them if they had seen anything of the Guards. When they said no, Birnie said that he was expecting the soldiers to arrive at any minute.

Unlike Stafford at the Oakley Arms, Birnie did not lead his men into action. Twenty minutes after Ellis and his party arrived, having evidently given up hope of any more reinforcements from the Office, Birnie called his force together. Acording to Ellis, 'some enquiries were made, but I don't know of whom, as to what number were likely to be in the room to which we were going, and whether Arthur Thistlewood was to be there.' Someone confirmed that Thistlewood was definitely in the building, and that he had about twelve men with him. Turning to Ellis, Birnie asked how many police were present.

The total was thirteen, not counting the magistrate. Birnie

* Not counting Gibbs, who was posted in the Pomfret Castle in Wigmore Street.

explained that as the soldiers were half an hour late, they had evidently lost their way, and the Bow Street party would have to act without them. Ellis replied that they would do the best they could, and Smithers said gamely that even if there were forty plotters in the stable, the police officers would still secure them.

Birnie sent someone to fetch Ruthven from the Horse and Groom.

*   *   *

After his encounter with Chapman and Lee in Molyneux Street, Thistlewood had gone down to Grosvenor Square to find out from Edwards what was stirring. The news was good : a number of carriages were setting down on the south side of the square, as if a party or a rout were in progress. Thistlewood at once assumed that these carriages were taking Ministers to number thirty-nine, though in fact they were taking dinner guests to the Archbishop of York's, Lord Harrowby's next-door neighbour. Thistlewood hurried back to Cato Street, where he arrived shortly after seven o'clock.

In the stable Ings and Davidson, both heavily armed, stood on guard.* In the candle-lit hayloft there were perhaps fourteen men sitting round the carpenter's bench. Presently Ings was heard talking to someone below, then the heavily-built Tidd came up the ladder, followed by Monument.

At this stage, according to Robert Adams, 'some of the strange men that there were in the room began to find out what they were met for, and some said that it would be impossible with the men there was in the room to undertake it.' Tidd agreed with them, and insisted that it was no use going to Lord Harrowby's with less than forty men. Thistlewood, however, was determined to carry on, and warned, 'If we drop the thing now, it will turn out another Despard's Job.' The excitable Ings acted like a madman, stamping his feet and swearing.

Brunt said that perhaps the doubters did not realise how easily the Ministers could be killed with the weapons available; they had things prepared, he claimed, 'which would soon destroy the Buggers'. Thistlewood pointed out that they were twenty

---

* Davidson later went up into the loft, leaving Ings on guard by himself.

strong,* which was quite enough; even if there were sixteen
servants at Lord Harrowby's house, it made no difference, because they would be taken by surprise. Six men could take care of
them, leaving fourteen to kill Harrowby and his guests. The
whole business could be done in ten minutes.

Aided by Brunt, Thistlewood began to choose the men who
would go into the dining-room. The gin bottle made its appearance, says Adams, and 'went round very brisk'. Suddenly there
was a noise in the stable below, and a voice called out 'Holloa,
hold a light.' Looking confused, Thistlewood held up a candle to
see what was happening. A man holding a pistol appeared at the
head of the ladder, and Adams claimed he heard him say,
'Here's a pretty nest of it! Gentlemen, we have got a warrant to
apprehend you all, and hope you'll go peaceably.'

*   *   *

At a quarter to eight that night the picquet guard at Portman
Barracks was paraded, issued with twenty rounds of ball cartridge per man, and marched off under the command of Lieuten-
ant Frederick Fitzclarence : three NCOs and thirty men of the
Second Battalion Coldstream Guards. Fitzclarence did not tell
them where they were going, or why, but they assumed that a
fire had broken out in the neighbourhood and that, as was quite
common on such occasions, they were going to protect the
property from looters.

Arriving in John Street, Fitzclarence looked in vain for the
Horse and Groom, so he ordered a halt and sent his servant, John
Mansfield, to scout forward. Mansfield found the public house
without much trouble and reported back to Fitzclarence; then
the two of them walked along John Street until Mansfield was
able to point it out. Returning to his men, Fitzclarence ordered
them to fix bayonets, shoulder arms, and keep strict silence. The
party then moved on again. After a few paces they heard the
sound of firearms and Fitzclarence ordered 'Advance, double
quick time.' As they doubled forward a tall man with a lazy eye
emerged from the archway which led into Cato Street and
walked past them. No one took any notice of him.

* He probably included Edwards in this total.

A few minutes earlier, Birnie had told Ruthven to clear the stable, and the Bow Street force went impressively into action. As Ruthven thrust his way into the stable, the first thing he saw was a man walking backwards and forwards like a sentry, carrying a gun on his shoulder and a sword at his side.

'What sort of man was that?' he was asked afterwards.

'I cannot say, for I did not stop one instant. I said to the party with me "Secure that man!" and went up stairs.'

Someone hit Ings in the eye and knocked him to the ground, while Ellis, Surman and Smithers went up the ladder after Ruthven. In the flickering candlelight of the loft Ruthven saw shabbily-dressed men sitting round a bench which was covered with jugs of beer, loaves of bread, bayonets and cutlasses, pistols and sword-belts, daggers and cartridges. Some of the men were eating and drinking, others were loading pistols or strapping on belts. Acording to Ruthven, he never made the remark quoted by Adams, but said, 'We are peace officers. Lay down your arms.'

There were cries of 'The bloody Traps are come!' and 'Throw the buggers downstairs!'

Ruthven had no difficulty in picking out Thistlewood; 'I knew him as well as I knew my own father,' he said. He saw that Thistlewood was holding a cut-and-thrust type of sword which had an unusually long blade, rather bright. Fencing with it to keep the police off, Thistlewood began to back into one of the small rooms at the side of the loft. Ellis pointed a pistol at him and said, 'Drop your sword or I'll fire instantly!'

'Let *me* forward,' said Smithers and moved towards Thistlewood, who thrust him deep in the right breast.

'Oh God,' Smithers gasped. 'I am ... '

He staggered back against Ellis and slumped to the floor. Ellis and Ruthven both snapped pistols at Thistlewood, but Ellis fired wide and Ruthven's powder flashed in the pan. The candles on the bench were slashed out with swords.

When he first entered the stable, Gill of the Dismounted Horse Patrol had helped to secure Ings. Leaving him guarded by Westcott, Gill then started up the ladder behind Luke Nixon. He heard the sound of a pistol shot, and Ruthven's voice calling

'Send the soldiers up.' Then Ellis appeared at the top of the ladder shouting that there was no time to be lost, 'and he came down in such a hurry that he knocked down Nixon, and Nixon knocked down me, and I fell in the corner.' Picking himself up, Gill was swept out of the building in a rush of men.

Everything was now utter chaos, with police and plotters tumbling down the ladder and out in the street. The loft was in darkness, except when a pistol flashed, and full of smoke. There were several more cries of 'Kill the buggers!' as the plotters fell and scrambled down into the stable. 'Yes, kill the buggers!' said Ruthven, not anxious to be identified as a policeman just at that moment.

At the height of the confusion a local tailor named William Salmon had the misfortune to turn into Cato Street, just in time to hear someone shout 'Smithers is stabbed!' A moment or so later two men came out of the stable, one of them a tall thin man wearing a darkish coat and carrying a sword. Striking out at Salmon with the sword, the thin man cut him twice through the hat and once through the pantaloons. In the light of a street lamp opposite, Patrole Joseph Champion saw Thistlewood running fast down Cato Street, waving the sword in circles round his head, though no one was within yards of him. Champion ran after him, but Thistlewood vanished into the night.

When Ruthven had led into the stable, Chapman and Lee were still in Queen Street but they ran up when they heard the firing. They saw Davidson running towards John Street, carrying a sword and a carbine, pursued by Ellis and Gill. Ellis caught hold of the black under the archway.

'I catched him by the collar,' he said, 'and he attempted to cut at me, but I was too close to him.'

Gill then came up and hit Davidson on the wrist with his truncheon, at which the black cried out, 'Oh! I am lame, I am lame.'

'Damn your eyes,' Gill swore at him, 'I will cut your hand off.'

He then made a grab at the sword, but the blade was so sharp that it cut his fingers and he had to let go. With Chapman's aid, Davidson was finally disarmed and taken into a chandler's shop, singing 'Scots Wha Hae Wi' Wallace Bled' at the top of his voice.

As the Guards came doubling through the archway into Cato Street, Fitzclarence saw a police officer pointing to the stable and shouting 'Soldiers, soldiers, the doorway!' Sword in hand, and calling out 'Coldstreams, do your duty!' Fitzclarence dashed into the building. Ruthven was close behind him and shouted at Tidd, who was trying to get out into the street. Tidd raised his arm as if to fire.

'I catched hold of his arm,' said Ruthven, 'pulled him round, and fell with him on a dung heap.'

*   *   *

By now half of Thistlewood's men were scurrying through the back streets of Marylebone, and the Guards soon had the situation in hand. In the smoke-filled loft they found the corpse of Smithers. They also found Strange, Bradburn, Monument and Gilchrist hiding under piles of straw and shavings. The carpenter's bench was covered in scuff marks, made by the plotters' boots as they scrambled out of the loft.

Some had climbed through a skylight, and got away through adjoining houses or over the rooftops into Edgware Road. A few had squeezed through the openings in the floor of the loft, dropped into the mangers in the stable below, and run out into Cato Street. Ings only got as far as the Edgware Road, where he was tackled by two local watchmen, who held on to him until Brooks of Bow Street came up. Ings had fired at Brooks and slightly wounded him, which had put the Patrole in a temper. He told Ings that if he had had his sword with him, he would have cut off his head.

Several men named in the warrant had got clean away, including Thistlewood, Adams, Harrison and Brunt. Others whose names were not in the warrant had also escaped, though few of them were at liberty for long. Nine prisoners had been taken, mostly by the Guards; it seemed clear that the operation should have been led by John Stafford, who thoroughly understood such things. As it was, one officer was dead and another was badly wounded, a bullet having ploughed under Surman's scalp and emerged close to his ear. John Wright had been saved from a sword thrust by his unusually thick braces, Westcott's hat had three bullets in it, and a sword point had pierced Private Strickland's pantaloons and drawers.

The loft was cleared of its weird assortment of weapons, including the broomsticks fitted with second-hand files and a home-made grenade as big as Ruthven's hat. Then the Guards escorted the prisoners and the booty to Bow Street where, to add a final grotesque touch to the business, they arrived just as the Covent Garden theatres were emptying out. The extraordinary scene was vividly described by the *Courier*:

> The Police Office surrounded by the military, their arms gleaming in the glaring light of the torches, many of them carrying muskets and other spoils taken in the affray, the roar of the coaches in consequence of the Theatres being just closed, and the confused buz of the multitude drawn together by the appearance of the military, gave altogether a very un-English complexion to the night.

Mr. Birnie arrived at the Office at about 10 p.m. and gave a dramatic account of the action, in which he said he had narrowly escaped death, several shots having passed close to his head. He then took his seat on the bench, and there were put to the bar James Ings, Richard Tidd, William Davidson, Charles Cooper, Richard Bradburn, James Gilchrist, John Monument, James Wilson and John Shaw Strange. The Guards returned to Portman Barracks, carrying the weapons with them.

*　　　*　　　*

After taking over the watch in Grosvenor Square from Julian Thistlewood and Mrs. Tidd, George Edwards had passed a quiet evening. Several plotters called at the square on their way to the Horse and Groom, and Potter and two of his men also looked in. When Edwards asked Potter how things were progressing in Holborn, he replied that he thought it would be all right, but they were waiting to see what happened at Lord Harrowby's.

At about nine o'clock Thistlewood paid his second visit to the square. This time he was accompanied by a tall man and Brunt, who told Edwards that he had better be off.

'For why?' Edwards asked.

'We have been attacked,' Brunt answered, 'and have fought our way out.'

Thistlewood said that he had killed one of the Traps, a stout man, well-dressed and wearing black. He believed that it was Stafford. After Thistlewood had killed him, Brunt added, the lights were knocked out and 'there was nothing but pop, pop, pop.'

The four of them left the square and walked east. As described by Edwards, Thistlewood's manner was that of a general who had suffered a serious though by no means decisive reverse, his main concern now being to find out if the guns had been captured according to plan. Edwards told him about his talk with Potter and said he did not think that the artillery party had done anything. Thistlewood was surprised and angry, and explained that without the cannon there would be nothing left to rally on.

On their way through Soho they stopped to drink a glass of rum at a wine vault in Frith Street. Thistlewood insisted that they split up into pairs and use different doors, so as not to be too conspicuous.

When they came to Holborn he said angrily, 'See, there is nothing like a fire! What can that Palin have been at?'

At Middle Row he and the tall man went ahead to see if the guns were still at Gray's Inn Lane. Edwards and Brunt called at Fox Court, where Brunt told his wife to hide anything which might incriminate him. Afterwards, as they walked east towards the City, Harrison, Palin and Potter caught them up. They all went into a wine vault on Holborn Hill, where Palin got rather drunk. Later, as the five of them were going towards Smithfield, Palin threatened to shoot Edwards for betraying them. Pulling a brass-barrelled pistol from his pocket, Edwards showed it to Brunt and urged him to kill Palin. He also offered Brunt a swordstick and whispered, 'If you put him out of the world, we shall be safe.'

Palin went his own way and the others walked on to Chiswell

Street, where they were joined by Thistlewood. They strolled past the gates of the Artillery Ground and saw that everything there was normal.

'All's quiet here, too,' said Thistlewood. 'We have been sold by all parties.'

Edwards agreed that it was all up; they had been betrayed by 'the Mary-le-bone fellow'. Thistlewood did not know quite what to do or where to go, and seemed to be stunned by the realisation that there was not only nothing left to rally on, but no one left to rally. The *coup d'état* was a failure, another Despard's Job.

From Bunhill Row they walked up the City Road and into Leonard Street, apparently meaning to call on Cooke, who lived at the back of the Antelope in Holywell Lane. Crossing an open space they met Preston and several men they knew, including Murray and Harris's nephew.

'It's all up with us,' Thistlewood told them. 'Preston, you had best go home to bed.'

'Have you committed yourself?' Preston asked.

'Yes,' Thistlewood replied, 'deep enough.'

They all went into a public house in Willow Walk and ordered pints of beer. Thistlewood realised that he must soon find somewhere to hide; by next morning every spy and informer in London would be on the lookout for a 'middle-aged man about five foot ten, with a long face and sallow complexion, dark hair turning a little grey and a scar under the right jaw'.

He put the matter to Edwards, who, he said, had no cause to be afraid. 'You are all right, you are not known.'

Soon after this, Edwards took Brunt aside and told him, 'I must wish you a good night. I am going to conduct Thistlewood to a safe place.'

Leaving the public house, Edwards walked back towards Finsbury Square with Thistlewood, who said that he must wash Stafford's blood off his sword as soon as he got the chance. Presently they came to White Street and knocked at number eight, where Harris the Type Foundry foreman lived. Harris's wife told them he was not at home, so they waited. When he arrived Thistlewood told him, 'This is a terrible job. It has turned out so unfortunate that I must request an asylum.'

Edwards left them and walked up to Barbican, where Potter and the others were supposed to meet him. Brunt had already gone back to Fox Court, where the police arrested him next day.

*   *   *

For Mr. Birnie, the fact that the police raid at Cato Street had obviously been bungled was a blow, both to his ambition and his self-esteem; but for the Runners and Patroles at Bow Street the event had a silver lining. The morning after his escape Arthur Thistlewood weighed a thousand pounds.

On what should have been the first day of his thirty years of comfort, Thistlewood decided to have breakfast in bed. Mrs. Harris took him a basin of coffee and a plate of toast. George Edwards came to the house soon afterwards, and when Thistlewood asked him what he thought about his hiding-place, the spy replied that he did not think it was too safe. At this, Edwards claims, 'He said he could not move till the evening and begged me to come to him [then], but to die rather than be taken.' Before he left again, Edwards told Harris, 'You must keep Thistlewood until this evening. I shall send some friends to take him away.'

The friends whom Edwards sent to take Thistlewood away arrived a mere thirty minutes later – four Bow Street officers and six of the Patrol. Three Patroles took post at the front door and three more at the back; then Ruthven, Salmon, Lavender and Bishop entered the house very quietly, the street door being fortunately on the latch, and searched the upstairs rooms before Mrs. Harris knew what was happening. Finding no sign of Thistlewood, they came downstairs and tried to open the door opposite Mrs. Harris's sitting-room. It was locked.

Bishop ordered her to give him the key, and after some hesitation she obeyed. Knowing what a desperate and dangerous man he was dealing with, Bishop put the key gently in the lock and slowly opened the door.

There was holes in the window shutters which admitted light into the room. There was a turn-up bedstead just facing the door, the foot of which came very near the door. On my opening the door a man who was in bed directly put up his head from under the blankets. I saw by the light through the shutters that it was Thistlewood. I had my pistol and staff in my hand and immediately threw myself upon the bed upon him and I said, 'I am an officer from Bow Street. I have a warrant against you, Mr. Thistlewood,' and seized hold of his hands. He said, 'Sir, I shall make no resistance.'

Lavender, Ruthven and Salmon came in and Thistlewood was allowed to dress; meanwhile the officers searched in vain for his sword. He was handcuffed and taken by hackney coach to Bow Street, where he stated that he knew he had killed a man, and hoped that it was Stafford. Mr. Birnie examined him briefly, and sent him to Whitehall to appear before the Privy Council. While waiting for the Council to summon him, he drank some porter and asked which gaol he would be going to. He said he hoped that it would not be Horsham.

The inquest on Smithers, at which Ruthven, Ellis and West-cott gave evidence, was held in the Horse and Groom. It established that, in addition to the sword thrust which had killed him, Smithers had received a second sabre wound under his blade bone, and a pistol bullet cast from pewter was found deep in his shoulder. Evidently he had been stabbed and shot at while he lay dying on the floor of the loft.

The Coroner told the jury that all the men who had gathered in the loft were equally guilty of the murder, because the act of the one was the act of the whole. One juryman announced that he had a doubt in his mind and asked for guidance : had not the men in the loft a right to defend themselves, he said, after the officer Ellis had fired his pistol?

'Certainly not,' the Coroner replied.

*　　　*　　　*

While the police were busy with Thistlewood at 8 White Street, Mrs. Harris had slipped out of the house, presumably to run to the Type Foundry and warn her husband, who promptly vanished. Apart from Thistlewood, the only other people under her roof were Mrs. Hill, the lodger, and a man named Lewis Casper. Together with Mrs. Harris they were taken to Bow Street for examination.

Mrs. Harris said that Thistlewood had called to see her the previous morning, and asked after a lodging which she was advertising by a placard in her window. She told him that she wanted two-and-six a week for the lodging, and that if he took it he would have to share a bed with her nephew. Thistlewood agreed and went away, returning between ten and eleven that night, by which time she had almost given him up. He had gone straight to bed.

She denied that she had been harbouring him, and explained that the reason why his bedroom door had been locked was because there was something the matter with the catch, so that locking it was the only way you could keep it shut. Questioned about Lewis Casper, she said that until they were all put into the coach for Bow Street she had not even known that he was in her house.

Apparently he was an acquaintance of Mrs. Hill.

11

The Prisoners Examined

ONE BY ONE, on the twenty-fourth and succeeding days, those who had been arrested went before the members of the Privy Council with their explanations.

James Wilson had been going down Cato Street on Wednesday when a man whom he did not know had called him by name and asked him to take a glass of gin. The man said he wanted Wilson for something, and tricked him into going to the stable . . .

Richard Bradburn said that as he was coming from his lodgings he met Thistlewood, who told him that he would be welcome at a dinner which had been arranged at the Horse and Groom. When Bradburn asked what it was for, Thistlewood said he would tell him when he got there. The upshot was that he found himself in a stable 'with a parcel of old things lying about'.

He drank some of the beer that had been provided, then tried to leave, but the sentries at the door would not let him. There was a tall man in a green coat who gave him some pistol balls and told him to use them, but he threw the best part of them on the floor and hid. Unfortunately, six of the pistol balls were still in his pocket when he was arrested . . .

James Gilchrist had been looking for work when he met a little man he knew in the Horse and Groom. The man, Strange, was a clicker, and so belonged to the same trade as Gilchrist; that was how they knew one another. He said that he knew where they could get bread and cheese and beer, and Gilchrist thought he might as well have some, because he only had a halfpenny in his pocket and was very hungry.

So they went to the stable, not speaking to anyone on the way; Gilchrist just went straggling along with 'this little lad Strange'. At the stable he ate some bread and cheese, but he could not say who had paid for it. He had never been in company with any of the other men there, the only man he knew was Strange. While he was eating he asked them what they were going to be about, but they told him to fill his belly and he should see afterwards. Seeing the arms on the table, he asked what they were for, but no one would tell him.

When the police came he 'went backwards' with Strange, and the people 'began a-firing'. He got down on the floor, and a man lay down beside him and made heavy groans. This man was a Peace Officer, though he did not know it at the time. He just cowered him down out of the way . . .

Charles Cooper was still in bed on the twenty-third when Brunt and another man called and asked him if he would go to a meeting. He said he thought that the Six Acts had done away with meetings, but they explained that only public meetings were affected, not private ones.

They told him to be at the Horse and Groom after dusk, but when he got there he could see no sign of any meeting going on. He told the landlord that he had expected to meet a party of respectable people there. The landlord knew nothing about any such party. So Cooper left, but just as he was walking away he met a black man who showed him to the stable. The only man he knew there was Gilchrist, who was one of his fraternity.

What he saw in the loft struck him with horror: with all the arms lying about, the place put him in mind of a Banditti at the Playhouse.

'What's all this?' he asked.

'You see what it is,' they replied.

'Dear me,' said Cooper. 'What can all this be?'

When Thistlewood came he acted like a man who was drunk, saying that fifty men began the Revolution in France, so why should not fifty men do the same here? Cooper replied that he would not wish to be one of five hundred men for such a purpose, let alone fifty, and that they were all in a scrape. The

talk ran quite high. Thistlewood talked of the blood of Englishmen and asked if even cowards would not fight in a good cause.
He raved about taking guns and holding a position about Chalk
Farm, where the people would join him because they were all
ripe for it. Very few appeared to agree with him, though there
were four or five in the same mad state. Cooper did not know
their names, but the black man was one; he seemed to be a
resolute man. The butcher was another.

Thistlewood said that every man who would not stand by
him ought to be shot, at which witness began to feel that he was
in an awkward situation; he thought that Thistlewood would
shoot him if he tried to leave. He sat musing till the officers
came. When the Guards arrived he threw himself at the officer
for protection. He thought that the meeting was a trap, laid to get
the men into a scrape, and was afraid that the innocent would
suffer with the guilty . . .

John Firth admitted that he knew Thistlewood, but claimed
that he had never had any private conversation with him as he
did not like the man. He had gone home to his tea on Wednesday
at a quarter to six. Afterwards he went to his shed to do up
his cows, which he always did at seven, as regular as the clock
struck. At a quarter to nine he returned to 23 Bryanston Street,
where he lived; then he went along to Doctor Macdonnell's
in Orchard Street to get a draught for his wife, who had been
troubled with a stomach pain.

The doctor mixed up the draught and Firth took it back
home; it had 'Spirit of Lavender' written on the label. As he was
going along Oxford Street he heard the watchman saying 'Half
past eight'. At Bryanston Street he found a man named Gray
waiting at his door, and learned from him that there had been
firing at his stable. He went straight to John Street and saw a
crowd in the archway, but he was so horror-struck that he did
not go in. He went away and walked up and down Portman
Square in great agitation until half past ten, and did not go to
bed until midnight. He never was one inch nearer to Grosvenor
Square that night 'than the Kirb Stone on the right hand side
of Oxford Street' . . .

Tidd's story was that 'a certain man' took him to the Horse and Groom and afterwards to the loft, where he arrived only two minutes before the police raid. Brunt swore that he had never been in Cato Street at all; he was home that night at a little after nine.

Ings said that he had known that Brunt and a few others meant to strike a blow – they had talked of taking the Bank of England and dispatching Ministers. But they never told him any particulars, saying that when the time came they would let him know.

Thistlewood, warned that he stood accused of treason and murder, replied, 'I shall say nothing. I have only one thing to say : in the house that I slept at the person is quite innocent.'

*   *   *

While the Council was examining the prisoners, John Stafford was patiently interviewing the residents of Marylebone, especially those who lived in Cato Street or near to Lord's Old Cricket Ground. He was chiefly interested in their neighbours : a blacksmith who had not been seen since Wednesday, a shoemaker who had come home with a tear in his coat, a tinman who was friendly with Davidson the black.

On the twenty-fifth the police took up Robert Adams, Simmons the footman, and John Harrison. Harrison swore that he had hired the stable on behalf of a distiller named James McCarthy, who wanted to keep a still there. Harrison had gone to the loft just before the police raid, and seeing the arms strewn on the bench had told the plotters to remove them, as he was answerable for the place. Several of them ordered him to hold his tongue and threatened to blow his brains out.

Also arrested on the twenty-fifth was Thomas Hazard, the seventy-year-old teacher, who was so palsied that he had to be carried up the court-house stairs. Abel Hall, the Finsbury tailor, was arrested next day. On the twenty-eighth Preston was brought in, parting from his daughters with the remark that 'Lord Sidmouth could not get up the farce' without him.

A £200 reward was out for John Palin or Peeling – 'aged forty, stoops a little, round-shouldered, grey hair, five foot seven, scowling look.' Police officers called at Vine Yard, Southwark where he co-habited with a woman named Privett, but the only trace they could find of Mr. Palin was a pair of corduroy breeches. The search for him extended to the third floor room of a house in Pitt's Place, Great Wild Street. Here the police found James Wilson's wife and children, who had neither a fire nor bedding and were clearly starving. Samuel Waddington's premises were also searched by Bow Street officers, who seized a full length picture of him carrying a bundle of twopenny trash under his arm and blowing a horn; it was captioned 'Samuel Waddington, printer and publisher to the Radical Union.'[15]

Meanwhile the scene in Cato Street reminded Marylebone's older residents of the great days of the Tyburn hangings. From early morning till well after dark the place was like a fairground, with gentlemen of rank and elegant ladies rubbing shoulders with characters of the worst description. Sightseers packed the Horse and Groom and paid to visit the hayloft, where bloodstains could be seen upon the floor.

By this time a fund had been started for Smithers's widow and the police officers who had taken part in the raid, and a benefit performance was given at the Theatre Royal, Drury Lane. The subscribers included the Earl of Essex who remarked that, apart from the officers, there was another person engaged in the Cato Street affair who was above pecuniary reward, but still entitled to the warmest thanks of his country. He was referring to Mr. Richard Birnie.

In spite of his bad management, Birnie had been widely praised in the papers, which spoke of him fearlessly exhorting his men while the bullets whistled past his head. He had submitted to the Home Office a list of all the men who had taken part in the operation, with the observation, 'I consider the whole to have done their duty.' Against George Ruthven's name he wrote, 'I conceive stands alone on very high grounds.'

Police activity in and around Cato Street continued for some days more. A number of local people had reason to curse Thistlewood and his plot, including a grocer and cheesemonger named William Cannon, whose premises at 1 Molyneux Street were raided on 29 February. After breaking down two doors and smashing several pieces of furniture the police found one bullet mould, some iron shot flasks, a small printing press, half a pound of gunpowder and three dozen bottles of White Cape wine.[16]

The warrant to search Cannon's premises was one of the last ever signed at Marlborough Street by Robert Baker; early in March he was appointed Chief Magistrate to succeed Sir Nathaniel Conant and transferred to Bow Street. Mr. Birnie took the news very hard, complaining to a fellow magistrate, 'This is the reward a man gets for risking his life in the service of his country.' According to *The Gentleman's Magazine* he said it publicly on the bench, with tears in his eyes.

*   *   *

By the beginning of March eighteen men had been arrested for high treason, misprision of high treason, or suspicion of high treason. Thistlewood, Brunt and all the men taken at Cato Street were in Coldbath Fields. In Tothill Fields were Preston, Simmons, Harrison, Hazard, Hall and Firth. Robert Adams was being kept apart, for reasons which will become apparent.

For the people of London the public appearance of these men made good free entertainment; but for the authorities, who had to guard against escape and rescue attempts, it was a great strain.

The first of these ordeals occurred on 3 March, when the prisoners were taken before the Privy Council. For the men in Tothill Fields, who were deemed to have played relatively minor roles in the plot, it was only a few minutes' journey to Whitehall, but the more dangerous ones at Coldbath Fields had over two miles to go, through some of the poorest parts of the capital. Thistlewood and his fellow prisoners were handcuffed and guarded by three coachloads of Bow Street officers and Patroles.

Thistlewood looked yellowish in the face, and seemed thinner than ever. Preston was full of himself, as usual, and continued 'very talkative and lofty'.

He seemed bursting with impatience to go before the Council; raising himself from his chair every time the door opened, in hope of being the next called; then sinking back into his seat with vexation and disappointment, and exclaiming, 'Oh! how I long to go up! My *genus* is so great just now, I don't think there is any man alive has so great a *genus* as mine is at this moment.' Then he would pore upon the ground for a minute or two in deep cogitation; and at length break out into the following soliloquy: 'If it is the will of the Author of the World that I should perish in the cause of freedom – his will, and not mine, be done! It would be quite a triumph to me! Quite a triumph to me!' – at the same time throwing his arms about in a manner which savoured strongly of insanity.*

When the examination ended, Preston, Hazard and Simmons went back to Tothill Fields. Six more were sent to Coldbath Fields.† Thistlewood was committed to the Tower, together with Brunt, Ings, Tidd, Davidson, Wilson, Harrison and Monument. He refused to concede that the Establishment had won. 'I hear the Spaniards are getting on famously,' he told his companions, as they waited to go to the Tower. 'They'll all have it in their turn; they may scrag a few of us, but there is more going on than they are aware of.'

He was lodged in the Bloody Tower, in quarters said to have been occupied by Colonel Despard, and allowed to exercise on the leads, which commanded a fine view of the Thames and the Surrey hills. His wife was able to visit him, but she was thoroughly searched: even her stays had to be removed and examined, and her long black hair was unbound and combed out.

The hunt for Palin and other suspects went on, and on 5 March Robert George, the Lisson Green sailor, was taken up by Ruthven and Salmon in a Wapping tavern. 'He is a young man of very decent appearance,' announced the *Observer*, which was less generous towards Thomas Hazard. According to the paper, Hazard's house in Queen Street was crowded every night with the most intense Radicals, who pretended to be reading newspapers while plotting against the Government.

* George Theodore Wilkinson, op. cit.
† Bradburn, Strange, Gilchrist, Cooper, Hall and Firth. The two last-named were not tried.

On 13 March, at Bow Street, Mr. Birnie examined Thomas Chambers, who freely admitted to being a Radical reformer.

MR. BIRNIE : What do you mean by a Radical reformer?

CHAMBERS : Why, that I and every honest man should have a vote in electing those who make the laws respecting liberty, life and property.

MR. BIRNIE : Nonsense; it is all from this stuff being propagated that has caused all this disturbance in the country. Do you not think things of this sort had better be left to men of property and talent who have the administration of State affairs? For if they ruin the State they ruin themselves.

CHAMBERS : In some cases they might; but every man ought to have a vote.

There was an awkward moment when Chambers spoke of George Edwards visiting his house with some drunken men. 'We know all about that,' said Birnie sharply. 'We will speak of that afterwards.' Then, turning to Ruthven, he said, 'Edwards, I believe, is not in custody?'

'No, sir, I believe not,' Ruthven replied, and walked away to the other end of the room.

In spite of all the Government's red herrings and the production of Hiden and Dwyer, many people were convinced that Edwards was a spy. Otherwise, since his name had been on the warrant on the twenty-third, why was he still at liberty? According to *The Traveller*, one of his acquaintances had encountered him at the Old Bailey and tried to pump him, saying, 'George, you must have made a good thing of it, if you have got the £1,000.' Edwards had burst into a fit of laughter.

He seemed to be a particularly evil character, even for someone who lived off Blood Money. It was rumoured that just before betraying Thistlewood's hiding-place to Bow Street he had called on Susan Thistlewood and assured her that her husband was safe. Now, on the Crown list of witnesses for the forthcoming trials, he was described as 'George Edwards, Ranelagh Place, modeller', and though he had vanished from that address no doubt Bow Street knew where to contact him.

Alderman Wood, who was now Member of Parliament for the City, felt very strongly that Edwards should be produced in court, if only to give defence counsel a chance to discredit him. That was not the way the Government worked. The disastrous effect which Jack Castle had produced on Watson's jury in 1817 had taught the Law Officers of the Crown a sharp lesson. It was, for instance, why Oliver never made an appearance at the Derby trials that year, though he was kept hidden in the town in case he was needed. The last thing that the Attorney-General wanted was a repetition of the Westminster Hall fiasco; so when Robert Adams showed signs of wanting to turn king's evidence he was given every encouragement. Juries were much more likely to accept the evidence of an accomplice in custody than that of a paid spy.

The task of drawing out Adams's recollections and getting them into written form fell to John Stafford. Adams mentioned ten men he said he knew very well: Thistlewood, Brunt, Ings, Tidd, Davidson, Harrison, Bradburn, Wilson, Hall and Strange. He named seven more whom he knew less well, but whom he thought that he would still recognise if he ever saw them again. These seven were Preston, Cooper, Gilchrist, Monument, Hazard, George and Firth. Ten plotters, he added, were still at liberty.

There are six that were in the room at Cato Street not taken yet, besides Palin, Potter and Cooke.* By the calculation I have made there are nine not in custody. Harris makes the number ten. In my opinion four of the last-mentioned ten are more deserving of punishment than some of those in confinement; those four are Palin, Potter, Cooke and Harris, for they are all very much concerned in the plot. Some of the others I am sorry for, as they did not appear to know what they came for, but God only knows best about that.

* He said that, so far as he knew, these three were not present at Cato Street.

If any of them that belong to the set that are not yet taken should happen to know that I am going before the Grand Jury to testify the truth of what I have said, they would not care* to murder me if they see the least opportunity of doing it, for it is the system of the Radicals altogether.

Remembering how Watson's jury had balked at finding him guilty of high treason, when a charge of incitement to riot would probably have succeeded, some members of the Cabinet felt that the Cato Street gang ought to be tried for murder. They were advised that on a charge of murder a jury would probably find Thistlewood guilty and acquit all the others, so a charge of high treason was agreed on. As the Old Bailey sessions did not begin until 12 April and the Government was anxious to settle things as soon as possible, someone suggested that the conspirators should be tried by Special Commission. This proved impracticable, as the proceedings of such a Commission would automatically be suspended once a new term in the Court of King's Bench began. Finally, all agreed that was no use trying to cut corners, and that the trials must be held under the ordinary gaol delivery; meanwhile a special commission of oyer and terminer could find the bills of indictment.

The Grand Jury found bills for high treason against eleven of the accused, plus a bill for murder against Thistlewood and several bills for malicious shooting. The eleven were Thistlewood, Brunt, Ings, Tidd, Davidson, Harrison, Wilson, Bradburn, Cooper, Gilchrist and Strange.

These, then, were the hard-core members of the conspiracy : a butcher, a baker, a cabinet-maker, six cobblers, one carpenter and an ex-officer of militia. John Monument, whose committal to the Tower had unnerved him completely, was allowed to turn king's evidence.†

'I hope we shall have a convincing and convicting case,' Henry Hobhouse wrote to Sir John Byng.

---

* i.e. scruple.
† His brother Thomas also appeared as a witness for the Crown.

On 25 March Lord Sidmouth had audience of the King, lately returned from Brighton. Low in spirits and weak in body, His Majesty had recourse to laudanum before proceeding to business.

*   *   *

Lord Castlereagh was apparently so shaken by the revelation of Thistlewood's plot that he began carrying two loaded pistols about in his breeches pockets. One evening he produced these weapons at the dinner table at St. James's Square and showed them to his guests. For the rest of the meal the Russian Ambassador's wife sat sideways in her chair, terrified that the pistols would go off whenever Castlereagh made a move to offer her something. Edging away from her host, she got so close to her right-hand neighbour that he could hardly put anything in his mouth.

12

Adams Earns His Keep

THERE was an immense amount of paperwork to be done in the eight weeks which elapsed between the fight in Cato Street and the start of the trials. Apart from the usual bills, indictments, lists and writs, the depositions of 162 witnesses for the Crown had to be taken down and checked for discrepancies. Before the 1817 trials at Derby, any statement which seemed to need Oliver's confirmation was deleted; similar care had to be taken now with the Cato Street evidence, so that George Edwards could stay well out of sight. Everything had to be written out several times, and all the copies had to match. Four key witnesses had to be examined, prompted, recorded and frequently reassured. Adams had to be coached until he was not only quite sure of all the facts in his extremely long and vital deposition, but able to stick to them under cross-examination.

Thomas Hiden was appalled to learn that he would have to give evidence at the Old Bailey, and said that he would never dare go home again. Three days before the trials began, Hobhouse informed the Treasury Solicitor:

> He also appears to have something on his conscience as to having with-held much that he knows, and enquired with curiosity when his statement would be delivered to the Council. Mr. Day has seen him and endeavoured to quiet his fears.

Himself a former Assistant Treasury Solicitor and a barrister-at-law, Hobhouse had been studying Thistlewood's background, in which it had never been very easy to distinguish fact from rumour. Hobhouse knew that when Lord Sidmouth had taken legal action against Thistlewood in 1818, the Treasury advisers had been anxious to prove that Thistlewood had been 'in the military or naval service (if this was in fact true), or at least that he was, or pretended to be, of the rank of a gentleman.' Such proof, they contended, would help to establish Thistlewood's serious intention of fighting a duel with the Home Secretary, which his counsel were expected to deny.

It had been discovered then that Thistlewood had held a commission in the militia, but that he had not held it for very long. Now, in the spring of 1820, Hobhouse decided to find out why. A medical man named Marshall, formerly surgeon to the First West Yorks Militia, was traced to his home in Leeds, and at Hobhouse's request a Mr. Christopher Beckett called to see him. On 30 March Beckett wrote to Hobhouse that Marshall had not seen or heard anything of Thistlewood for twelve years, but remembered that he had been discharged from the First West Yorks for bad conduct. 'His associates afterwards are stated to have been ostlers, postboys and others of a similar description.'*

*   *   *

On 14 April the prisoners for trial were moved to England's best-known gaol. Just after half past six that morning a detachment of Life Guards arrived at the Tower, followed by a strong force of Bow Street officers and Patroles. Seven carriages had been hired for the prisoners.

They were all perfectly silent until about to depart, when they expressed their thanks to the Warder for the humane treatment which thy had received. The whole being now assembled, they were marched each between two Bow-street officers to the Fosse-gate, beyond which the carriages had been drawn up. Thistlewood was placed in the first carriage, and was joined by three police officers. The remaining prisoners were each placed in a separate carriage, and each

* Marshall either did not know, or had forgotten, that after serving in the First West Yorks Thistlewood had transferred to the Third Lincoln-shire.

attended by three Bow-street officers. They were accompanied by a troop of Life Guards, and proceeded in a direct
course to Newgate Prison. The carriages were flanked on
each side by Horse Guards in single file. Notwithstanding
the early hour of the morning, and the secrecy with which
the removal was so prudently conducted, as the carriages
issued from the Tower gates an immense throng had
assembled to witness their departure.

In the gaol of Newgate the Marshal's men and a large
body of constables were assembled at eleven o'clock for the
purpose of preserving order; and when, at twenty minutes
before eight, it was announced that the prisoners were
approaching, they sallied forth and formed a half-moon
in front of the Felons' Door. In a few seconds afterwards,
the Horse Guards turned the corner of the Old Bailey and
rode up to the prison.*

Later that day Bradburn, Strange, Gilchrist and Cooper
arrived from Coldbath Fields. Thistlewood was put in a small
cell by himself, and since the weather was still very cold he was
allowed a fire. He was guarded by one officer in the daytime and
by two at night.

On 15 April the prisoners were set to the bar at the Old
Bailey and pleaded not guilty to all the various indictments. Since
they severed in their challenges to the jury, the Crown was
obliged to try them one by one, and Thistlewood's trial began
two days later. While the jury list was being called over and the
prisoner was standing at the bar, a shabbily-dressed man went
to the dock before anyone could stop him, and put his hat on
the board in front of it; then, drawing Thistlewood's attention
to it, he motioned him to take something out.

The incident pointed to a disturbing laxity in the security
arrangements, since no one was supposed even to approach
Thistlewood without Lord Sidmouth's permission, let alone give
him anything. However, the damage was done : the man whom
Castlereagh described as 'a most desperate dog' put his hand

---

* George Theodore Wilkinson, op. cit.

inside the hat. Instead of the pistol or phial of poison which some people were expecting he drew out five oranges and stowed them in his pocket. He was immediately asked to hand them over to a turnkey, who took them away to be examined.

The trial lasted three days. On the second day, the Cold-streamers who had been at Cato Street lined up behind the witness box, carrying the weapons and explosives which had been taken in the raid and during the subsequent searches. One by one these exhibits were handed to Ruthven, who laid them out on a table.

A pike was screwed on a staff and handed to the Jury. The whole of the frightful apparatus was now exposed to view. Guns, blunderbusses, swords, pistols, pikes, sticks, cartridges, bullets; even the pot in which the tar was boiled – all were produced and identified.

The firearms remained loaded till produced on this occasion, when the charges were drawn; they were loaded with ball . . . The production of Ings's knife excited an involuntary shudder; it was a broad, desperate-looking weapon. The Jury inspected the arms separately, and particularly the pikes . . . The whole had a most formidable appearance.*

Sergeant Hanson of the Royal Artillery described the com-position of one of the grenades, which contained three and a half ounces of gunpowder and twelve pieces of iron. He also opened a grenade in front of the jury.

The pieces of iron principally consisted of old cart-nails, such as the tyres of wheels are nailed on with. The carcase, or tin-case, was wrapped in an old stocking, and the powder which it contained was pronounced very good.†

The system of trying the prisoners individually placed a great strain on Adams, the chief Crown witness, who had to tell his

* Wilkinson, op. cit.
† ibid.

story three times over in a week, giving evidence for eight hours
at Thistlewood's trial alone. He seemed afraid of losing the
thread of his narrative, and grew uneasy when Crown counsel
tried to lead him or asked an unexpected question. 'I will
mention it presently,' he would say, or 'If you will let me go on
in my statement . . . '

A curious thing happened when he was asked to name the
prisoners, who hissed him as he passed by. After identifying six
of them he was asked, 'Who is that short man, do you know
him?'

It was the little clicker, John Shaw Strange, listed by Adams
as one of the men whom he knew very well.

'I cannot say that I can swear to the man,' he answered. 'I
have seen him.'

'Now the other man, who is that?'

It was Richard Bradburn, the carpenter, who was also on
Adams's 'well-known' list. He was a remarkably good-looking
young man, not easily forgotten, and Adams had mentioned
him several times in his deposition. It was Bradburn who had
been sent to buy ferrules for the pike staves, and who boasted
that after Castlereagh's head had been cut off he would like
to take it in a box to Ireland. Furthermore, Adams had stated
that he had attended the Fox Court meeting on 20 February.

'I do not know his name,' Adams replied.

The Solicitor-General ordered three men whom Adams had
not been able to identify to be brought forward, and Strange,
Bradburn and Gilchrist moved to the front of the dock. Still
Adams could not name them.

'I have some recollection of *him*,' he said, gazing at Bradburn.
'But to swear to him, I cannot.'

For the defence, Mr. Curwood told the jury that they could
give no credence at all to Adams, 'who stood confessed the
betrayer of his companions, a traitor to his king, a rebel against
his country, an apostate to his religion, and a scoffer to his God.'
The jury were also warned about Hiden, another key Crown
witness, who had been in both the King's Bench and the
Marshalsea for debt; and a Marylebone cow doctor's apprentice

was produced who swore that Thomas Dwyer was not to be believed upon his oath.

This man, whose name was Edward Huckleston, said that he had been in very poor circumstances when he met Dwyer, who told him that he could put him in possession of many a bright pound and took him to Hyde Park.

> He told me to keep within hearing, and he would soon shew me how he could go on – that he would watch a gentleman out, and to catch hold of him, and that he would say that he was an unnatural gentleman, and that then I was to come up as an officer, and draw him towards a watch-house, but not to take him to a watch-house . . . He said that he got £10 of one gentleman in Saint James Street, by only catching hold of him by the collar.

*   *   *

Thistlewood's trial was notable for the brilliant performance of John Adolphus, his leading counsel. According to his daughter,* Adolphus was utterly loyal to the Crown and had a thorough hatred of traitors, but he never allowed it to affect his pleadings for them. For traitors, as for any other clients, he used his considerable talents to the full.

He had sat up all night before the trial began, digesting the mass of evidence. As he told the jury, Thistlewood's trial had started on a Monday, and he had not been chosen to represent him until the previous Thursday; and unavoidable business had kept him out of town for the whole of Friday. He had received no instructions from Thistlewood and no information. All he knew of the case was through materials which Mr. Harmer, solicitor for the defence, had been able to collect over the last few days.

Thistlewood, he told the jury, was a doomed man, being charged with both treason and murder. The only uncertain thing about his fate was whether his sentence would end with his decapitation, or whether his corpse would then be handed to a

---

* Emily Henderson, *Recollections of the Public Career and Private Life of the Late John Adolphus,* 1871.

surgeon for dissection. He said that he did not doubt that
Thistlewood had killed Smithers, and had planned to murder
the Cabinet, but he believed that his object was plunder, not
revolution.

Cross-examining Ruthven, who stated that he had known
Thistlewood since 1817, Adolphus tried hard to establish a
connection between Bow Street Public Office and George
Edwards.

Q. When had you seen Thistlewood last before this transaction on the 23rd of February – stop a moment before
you look to your book – had he been out of sight for
some time?

A. No, not a fortnight certainly.

Q. Had he lately been imprisoned to your knowledge?

A. No, not that I know of.

Q. I mean at Horsham?

A. I have heard of that.

Q. Do you know how long he had been come back from
Horsham?

A. No, I do not.

O. Had you seen him several times before the 23rd of
February?

A. I had seen him more than five or six times within two or
three weeks.

Q. Perhaps you had some particular motive for looking
after him at this time?

A. I had.

O. A motive connected with this event that took place
afterwards?

A. Not that I am aware of.

Q. I mean watching some proceedings, the end of which
was this meeting in Cato Street?

A. Not that I am aware of, I was watching him for another
purpose, as I believe.

Q. Do you know a man of the name of Edwards?

A. I do not.

Q. Is there an officer in your office that has a relation of
    that name?
A. We have I believe four or five Edwardses; but I am not
    aware what relations they have.

Adolphus hinted that it was not only his superiors at Bow
Street who had employed Ruthven to 'look after' Thistlewood.

Q. Upon whose suggestion that was, except those who
    employed you at the office, perhaps you do not know?
A. I do not.
Q. You have seen this person to whom I allude, named
    Edwards, since the 22nd of February?
A. I do not know the person to whom you allude.

Bishop, the officer who had captured Thistlewood, was asked
how he had got the address of the hiding-place at White Street.

Q. Was it from a Mr. Edwards?
A. No.
MR. GURNEY : I should have objected to that question.
LORD CHIEF JUSTICE DALLAS :* That is not a proper
    question.
WITNESS : I do not know a person of that name.
MR. ADOLPHUS : I should not have asked it if I had con-
    sidered it irregular; but the moment your Lordship gives
    that intimation I stop.
L. C. J. DALLAS : If these questions are to be asked it will
    break down all rules.
MR. ADOLPHUS : I submit, my Lord, to the intimation of
    your Lordship's opinion.

*   *   *

Since the indictment charged the plotters with conspiring against
the person and Government of King George IV, Adolphus questioned whether it was proper for Crown witnesses to repeat conversations which had taken place in the reign of George III. On
a more practical level, he said that the bags which were allegedly
for carrying off the severed heads of Sidmouth and Castlereagh

* Lord Chief Justice of the Court of Common Pleas.

were too small to hold them, and claimed that as a butcher Ings would have realised this. In any case, said Adolphus, it was incredible that a man so poor as Ings would have planned to encumber himself with two such unprofitable objects, when there were far more saleable things to be put into bags at 39 Grosvenor Square. He asked the jury to recall the gang's declarations of poverty, and suggested that the real purpose of the bags, which were produced in court, was to carry away Lord Harrowby's valuables. He could find no evidence that the meeting in Cato Street was connected with a plot to overthrow the Government.

What were the means they had prepared? A certain number of arms, barely sufficient for an expedition on the highway . . . by seizing cannon, eight in number – by conveying them without horses – by acting with them without any ammunition – by attacking the Mansion House, and in order to make this formidable attack on the Mansion House they place themselves at the greatest possible distance : in order to seize cannon in Gray's Inn Lane, they remove from Brook[e]'s Market, in the very neighbourhood, to the very farthest extremity of London, and having performed what they call the West End Job, they are to transport themselves to the Mansion House, a distance of nearly four – or, as they were to proceed – of five miles; two miles and a half before they can seize the first of those cannon, another mile and a half before they got the rest of those self-moving cannon, and another mile before they place them north and south, to attack the palace of the chief magistrate of the City; they are to make the cannon follow them as tamely as animals wanting their daily repast follow their keepers; and to do it with the more facility, they place themselves at the greatest possible distance from the scene of action.

The Attorney-General had already predicted what form the defence would take. He believed that Thistlewood's counsel would try to convince the jury that the alleged plot to take over the country was too absurd to be taken seriously, and had never existed; and for five hours, with tremendous style but uneven arguments, Adolphus tried to do just that.

> They were to do a great deal, they were to secure London against the troops, command the road between London and Windsor, and to cause a diversion and take possession of the telegraph at Woolwich, for fear some information should be conveyed to the ports. Thus were roads to be commanded in this direction; important diversions to be operated in that; telegraphs secured over the water; a metropolis like London secured, and an army paralyzed, by a band of five and twenty paupers, who, in addition to their other wonder-working facilities, must have possessed the gift of ubiquity . . .
>
> Gentlemen, what was to be done next; business multiplies upon us fast; we have done a pretty good stroke of work already; but another thing must be effected, we must get possession of several out-ports, Dover, Brighton, Ramsgate and Margate, and prevent any persons from leaving England without a licence. Very fine indeed! I wonder they omitted Harwich . . .

A traitor, he reminded the jury, was someone who levied war against the King; so even if Thistlewood really had formed the ludicrous idea of capturing the Bank, the Mansion House and those six pieces of cannon, Adolphus doubted that he could be charged with treason.

> The cannon are not the King's. Those at Gray's Inn Lane belong to the Body of Light Horse Volunteers, those in the Artillery Ground to a private company; the seizing of those is a felony, but not Treason; nor is the Mansion House one of the King's palaces; it is the official residence of the Lord Mayor; nor is the Bank the King's, it is the house of a chartered company.

Therefore, said Adolphus, the prosecution would have to prove

that Thistlewood and his band meant to set up a Provisional
Government, and the only evidence of this intention was the
Proclamation penned on the twenty-second [of February], evi-
dence which defence counsel did not take very seriously. As Mr.
Curwood put it :

A Provisional Government! Who was at the head of it?
Nobody! Who are the officers under it? Nobody! How is it
to be managed? No-one can tell! Where is the Provisional
Government sitting? You are left to find that out. All which
the world is told is that Mr. Ings, the pork-butcher, is the
secretary of the new Provisional Government.

Mr. Curwood endorsed his colleague's opinion that the conspiracy to overthrow the Government was a myth.

Where was this great conspiracy concocted? In a two-pair
back room! Where was the battle fought? In a stable!
Where were the traitors incorporated? In a hay loft! How
were they armed? With a few rusty swords, halberts, and
old pistols!

For a leader who had put the lives of ten other men in jeop-
ardy, Thistlewood took little enough interest in the proceedings.
He was found guilty on two out of the four counts : conspiring to
levy war and levying war against the King. On the latter count,
as Hobhouse noted in his diary, he was clearly innocent.

Ings was found guilty of conspiring to depose the King and
conspiring to levy war against him. The man who had been so
keen to kill Castlereagh cut a sorry figure in the dock, sobbing
that he had been 'sold like a bullock in the market' and putting
all the blame on Edwards.

The Attorney-General knows the man. He knew all their
plans for two months before I was acquainted with it.
(*Still crying*) When I was before Lord Sidmouth, a gentleman said Lord Sidmouth knew all about this for two

months. (*Still in tears*) I consider myself murdered if this man is not brought forward. (*A more violent gush of tears*) I am willing to die on the scaffold with him. He has told of everything which he did himself . . . I have a wife and four children.*

He tried to give his judges a piece of paper which he said would prove his character, adding pathetically, 'A gentleman put it down from my childhood,' but Sir Robert Dallas refused to take it. 'Witnesses to character must give their evidence upon oath,' he said.

It was left to the ugly little Brunt, 'the little man with a twist in his nose',† to give some dignity to the proceedings. Speaking of Castlereagh and Sidmouth, he said :

I conspired to put them out of the world, but I did not intend to commit High Treason. In undertaking to kill them and their fellow ministers, I did not expect to save my own life, but I was determined to die a martyr in my country's cause.

He had been deeply influenced by the Peterloo Massacre and a desire to avenge it. 'I think the circular issued by Lord Sidmouth was nothing but a thing sent out to instigate the cavalry to murder those men at Manchester, and if a man murders my brother I have a right to murder him.'

Adams was particularly hard on Brunt, claiming that when they worked together in France Brunt had used the name Thomas Morton, and was supposed to have left England because he was in trouble over forged Bank notes. He was a lazy man, Adams said, and treated his assistant badly; also he was 'very indecent' in front of Mrs Adams, and 'made use of the pot while she was in the room'. Adams also testified that at one of Thistlewood's meetings Brunt had said that if any police officers entered the room they should be murdered, and he would take good care

* Wilkinson, op. cit.
† Dwyer's description.

that it should not be found out. This was too much for Brunt,
who appealed to the bench.

> BRUNT : My Lord, can the witness look me in the face, and the
> jury, and state that?
>
> ADAMS : I can, with a good conscience.
>
> BRUNT : Then you are a bigger villain than I took you for
> before.
>
> LORD CHIEF BARON RICHARDS : You will be at liberty to say
> anything you choose by and by, but you should not inter-
> rupt the examination.
>
> SOLICITOR-GENERAL : Look at the jury, and state whether that
> is a fact?
>
> ADAMS : It is the fact, and you know it yourself, Brunt.
>
> LORD CHIEF BARON RICHARDS : Do not get into conversation
> with the prisoner.

Questioned by Brunt's counsel about Edwards, Adams said
that he had been in the plot from the beginning, and was 'very
busy' in making the grenades. Once he pulled a pair of pistols
from his pocket, and Adams heard him boast that he never went
anywhere without them.

Since Adams claimed that he had wanted to put a stop to the
conspiracy, Mr. Curwood asked him why he never reported it to
the authorities.

> A. I wished to save the trouble of being exposed in this sort of
> way.
>
> Q. You wished to save the trouble of these trials here?
>
> A. Yes.
>
> Q. And you wished to save the interference of the officers?
>
> A. Yes, you do not believe I am such a fool as not to wish that.
>
> MR. CURWOOD : No, I do not take you to be a fool, I assure
> you.

While Brunt's trial was in progress someone warned Henry
Hobhouse that Thistlewood might commit suicide. On 25 April
Hobhouse wrote to Sheriff Rothwell :

I yesterday received an intimation that an attempt was likely
to be made by Thistlewood's friends to convey Poison to him
in Newgate, and I have to-day heard from a different Quarter that the mode of effecting it is to be by leaving with him
a book of which the leaves are to be medicated with a Prep-
aration of Arsenic.

Hobhouse ordered that the turnkeys should never take their
eyes off Thistlewood for an instant during visits from his wife
and son, who must on no account be allowed to give him anything. The same day Hobhouse wrote to Byng :

Brunt has made no defence in Evidence at all, and I hope
will be convicted this afternoon. If so there can be little
doubt of convicting all the other Principal Conspirators.

After being out for only ten minutes, the jury found Brunt
guilty on the same two counts as Thistlewood. The defence then
put out feelers for a 'compact', suggesting that the remaining
eight defendants should change their pleas to guilty in exchange
for their lives. According to Hobhouse neither the Attorney-
General nor the Solicitor-General had any strong objection to
this – in fact they rather welcomed the idea. If the proceedings
dragged on through eight more trials, they feared that the witnesses would be exhausted and unable to stand cross-examination.

Several members of the Cabinet saw some wisdom in this, but
so far as Tidd and Davidson were concerned Lord Sidmouth
absolutely refused his consent. There could be no compact for
these two, he insisted; they must hang.

Tried together, they were convicted of conspiring to levy war
against the King. The last six prisoners then changed their pleas
to guilty, and Gilchrist made a moving speech, in which he described how he had been lured to Cato Street by the promise of
bread and cheese. 'I now stand here convicted of high treason,'
he said, 'after I served my King and country for twelve years.'
Finally he broke down and sobbed.

On 28 April they were all sentenced to hang : 'afterwards your heads shall be severed from your bodies, and your bodies be divided into four quarters, to be disposed of as His Majesty shall think fit.' The sentences on Harrison, Wilson, Bradburn, Strange and Cooper were subsequently commuted to transporation for life, while Gilchrist was reprieved until inquiries could be made about his character. For the five men due to hang, the quartering of the bodies was remitted.

Doctor Watson was still in prison for debt. As soon as he heard that Thistlewood was condemned to die, he wrote to Lord Sidmouth asking if he might be allowed to visit his old friend, and offered to pay the expenses of a police escort from Whitecross Street to Newgate. Alderman Wood also wanted to visit Thistlewood, mainly in order to find out more about George Edwards's role in the conspiracy. At the end of April, having heard a rumour that Edwards was planning to go to America, Wood wrote to Sidmouth urging him to stop the spy leaving England. Sidmouth replied, 'I know of no grounds which would justify me in issuing a warrant against Edwards, that being the only mode by which I could comply with your request.'

The Home Secretary was preoccupied with arrangements for the executions, and with plans for controlling the vast crowd which a 'hanging morning' never failed to attract. It seemed likely that Thistlewood and his friends would draw the biggest audience since the Reverend Doctor Dodd, author, felon and clerk in Holy Orders, had been hanged at Tyburn, and to complicate matters there were strong rumours that a rescue attempt would be made. Plans for erecting the gallows on the roof of the prison were considered, but finally abandoned.

*   *   *

On the last day of April, which was a Sunday, Henry Angelo the fencing-master dined out in the City. On his way home he saw that there was a crowd at Saint Sepulchre's and lights outside Newgate, where a scaffold was going up by torchlight in front of the Debtors' Door. He stopped to talk with a man who was offering window seats at a guinea each.*

* *The Reminiscences of Henry Angelo,* 1830.

'What!' said Angelo. 'To see four men have their heads cut off? I'll give you half a crown a head.'*

After some haggling the man took Angelo up to a garret where several other spectators were settling down to a game of cards. There was an unfounded rumour that the hangings would begin at seven, an hour earlier than usual; so having paid his entrée, Angelo meant to go home to the West End and return to claim his seat at six. The card players warned him that he would never be able to get through the crowds.

Deciding to stay the night and make the best of it, Angelo took a hand in the game and won nineteen shillings.

* The true number was five.

13

The Fate of Traitors

By 5 A.M. ON 1 May the streets and pavements round Newgate
Prison seemed to be paved with heads, and part of the railing of
Saint Sepulchre's Church had collapsed under the pressure of so
many bodies. Sightseers crowded the windows and packed the
roofs of every building for hundreds of yards around, and the
best window seats had sold for as much as two guineas each.

In Fleet Lane and the other adjoining streets a double row of
rails had been set up to keep the spectators at least two hundred
yards away from the gallows, but the crowd had ignored them.
When the City Marshals arrived soon after five they ordered the
space inside these rails to be cleared, and as soon as this had been
done the area was lined with police. About an hour later troops
arrived to take up position towards Saint Sepulchre's and Ludgate Hill.

The security arrangements were as perfect as only long practice could make them. Excluding the hidden mounted reserves,
which were horsed and ready to ride out from a dozen places,
there were four detachments of the Life Guards, the Light Horse
Volunteers, a hundred infantrymen from the Tower, the Sergeants and Corporals of both regiments of London Militia, and a
strong force of police and firemen. Placards inscribed 'The Riot
Act has been read – Disperse immediately' were ready to hand,
and the Lord Mayor had instructions to send regular reports
direct to Lord Sidmouth. Six pieces of horse artillery were posted
at Blackfriars Bridge, and the Twelfth Lancers had been ordered
up from Hounslow to the Queen's Riding House at Pimlico.

Shortly after seven o'clock the executioner appeared on the
scaffold, which was draped in black, and positioned the portable

steps which he would need when the time came to tie the ropes to the gallows beam. A block was brought out and put near the five coffins, which were thickly strewn with sawdust to soak up the blood. About twenty minutes later the prisoners were taken one by one into the Press Yard, a small enclosure in front of the Debtors' Wing, to have their irons knocked off and their arms pinioned. The first to arrive was Thistlewood, very pale but perfectly calm and composed. Looking up at the sky he remarked, 'It appears fine.'

While his fetters were being removed, Alderman Wood approached and insisted on putting questions to him, despite strong objections from one of the sheriffs. Questioned about his first meeting with Edwards, Thistlewood replied that it had taken place 'about June last' at Preston's.

'Preston in Lancashire?' Wood asked.

'No, Preston the shoemaker,' Thistlewood replied.

Asked if Edwards had ever given him money, he said, 'Yes, I had a little from him, a pound note at a time.'

On his way to the scaffold, Thistlewood was hailed by a reporter, who said that he would be happy to take down his remarks for the benefit of the public, but Thistlewood ignored him.

While the prisoners were being taken up to the scaffold, an officer of the Life Guards rode from Newgate to the detachment at Bridge Street, led it to join the picquet on Ludgate Hill, then ordered the combined force into line facing the Old Bailey. The flying artillery at Blackfriars Bridge formed a crescent across the road, with the guns pointing towards the bridge.

On the scaffold the executioner fixed the ropes round the prisoners' necks and pulled white nightcaps over their heads, while Davidson ceaselessly murmured prayers, apparently in the belief that God might stop the awful thing that was happening to him. Ings unsuccessfully tried to hide his fear under a show of bravado which many people, including at least two of his companions, found distasteful.

'Come, my old cock o' wax,' he cried to Tidd, 'keep up your spirits; it all will soon be over.' And to the executioner, 'Now, old Gentleman, finish me tidily. Pull the rope tighter, it may slip.'

Both Tidd and Thistlewood asked him not to make so much noise.[17]

Brunt's self-esteem and his hatred of the Government sustained him to the end. 'Soldiers!' he said scornfully. 'What do they here? I see nothing but a military government will do for this country.' When his neck-cloth was taken off the stiffener fell out. He looked down at it, then kicked it away, saying, 'I shan't want that any more.' Although his hands were bound, he contrived to push up his nightcap and took a last pinch of snuff.

To Tidd, Thistlewood said, 'We shall soon know the last grand secret.'

The drop fell at six minutes past eight. English hangmen still used a riding knot and a short, uniform drop, making no allowance for the subject's weight; consequently it was usually the heavily-built ones who 'passed' quickly, while the slimmer ones struggled as they choked and had to have their legs pulled. According to *The Traveller* :

> The executioner, who trembled much, was a long time tying up the prisoners; while this operation was going on a dead silence prevailed among the crowd, but the moment the drop fell, the general feeling was manifested by deep sighs and groans.

The agonies of death, says Wilkinson, were seen 'in their most terrific form'. Eyewitness accounts of this kind, harrowing as they are to read, help to illuminate the darker and sometimes forgotten side of George IV's England.

> Thistlewood struggled slightly for a few minutes, but each effort was more faint than that which preceded; and the body soon turned round slowly, as if upon the motion of the hand of death.
>
> Tidd, whose size gave cause to suppose that he would 'pass' with little comparative pain, scarcely moved after the fall. The struggles of Ings were great. The assistants of the executioner pulled his legs with all their might; and even

then the reluctance of the soul to part from its native seat
was to be observed in the vehement efforts of every part of
the body. Davidson, after three or four heaves, became mo-
tionless; but Brunt suffered extremely, and considerable ex-
ertions were made by the executioners and others to shorten
his agonies.*

A young gentleman who was watching from a building opposite, and who had never seen a hanging before, had to turn
his eyes away. In the same room was a pretty young woman,
'very decent-looking', who took the greatest interest in what was
happening and remarked, 'There's two of them not dead yet!'
The Traveller continues :

Ings and Brunt were those only who manifested pain while
hanging. The former writhed for some moments; but the
latter for several minutes seemed, from the horrifying con-
tortions of his countenance, to be suffering the most excru-
ciating torture. It was said that two of their associates were
seen upon the top of one of the houses by some of the Police,
who were upon the alert to take them.

Half an hour or so after the drop had fallen the bodies were
cut down and laid out in the coffins. A man wearing a black mask
climbed up to the platform to cut off the heads. It was said that
he was a body-snatcher who had been paid £20 for the occasion,
and that he was the man who had decapitated Despard in 1803.
Whoever he was, he knew what he was doing. Moving the block
to the head of each coffin in turn, he severed the heads with a
knife :[18] 'a most sanguinary and appalling sight,' wrote Henry
Angelo.

The crowd hooted and hissed as one by one, according to
custom, the dripping heads were held up while the traitors' names
were shouted out. Normally they were seized by the forelock, but
Tidd's had to be lifted two-handed by the cheeks, because of his
receding hairline. Davidson's bled profusely. Brunt's was acci-

* George Theodore Wilkinson, op. cit.

dentally dropped, and people howled with disgust and fury as it rolled about on the scaffold.

At nine o'clock the coffins were carried into the prison, and the crowd began to disperse. A serious disturbance was now unlikely and an hour later the troops marched off to barracks. Isolated acts of vengeance were still a possibility and a strict watch was kept that day on anyone who loitered near the Houses of Parliament.

*   *   *

Connecting Newgate Prison with the Old Bailey was a narrow flagged passage twenty yards long by eight feet wide. Several of the flags had been taken up, and a portion of the earth below removed to make a shallow trench. At about seven o'clock that evening the five coffins, which had been topped up with unslaked lime, were lowered into the trench and covered over with earth. The flags were then put back into place, and on one wall of the passage the letters T B I D T were cut.

Ignorant of these arrangements, the five widows were hoping to claim their husbands' remains for burial. Susan Thistlewood also tried to obtain a lock of Thistlewood's hair, and a book belonging to him which the Home Office had confiscated. She was told that her husband was already buried, and that all his property was forfeit because of his attainder.

At 11 p.m. on 1 May the five men sentenced to transportation were double-ironed and put into the Portsmouth coach, accompanied by the Clerk of the Papers and three well-armed guards. When they arrived at Portsmouth next morning they were taken aboard a hulk lying in the harbour, and in the afternoon transferred to the transport *Guildford*, due out from Spithead with 200 convicts for Botany Bay.

During his imprisonment, Cooper and a man named Irwin had had a brief conversation which someone took the trouble to write down and report to the Home Office. To judge by the spelling, the transcript at the Public Record Office is the original.

IRWIN : Well Charles, how do you do, you must have been Drunk that evening.

COOPER : No I was not. I was as sober as I ham now.

IRWIN : But what damn Fools you must have been, their was no Cabinett dinner that Day – I was solicited but did not like the Party – I very nigh got myself into a nice little hobble through it.

COOPER : They ought to trace it to the heads of it.

IRWIN : Those things must be sifted – and if it all comes out things will be dicorous in Parliament.

COOPER : Adams will get a good bit of money by it.

IRWIN : Such people as them don't deserve anything for their Noseing, nothing is bad enough for them – but Sheriff Parkins as taken it in hand and says he will spend Two Thousand Pounds to see you all righted.

COOPER : I don't want him to do anything for me – but I could put him a bit to rights if I like.

Not long afterwards a medical student named Thomas Davies went home to his lodging carrying a human head, the property of Saint Thomas's Hospital, intending to dissect it at his leisure. The head was seen by several people, and a rumour spread that Davies was the masked man who had decapitated the Cato Street conspirators. Some days later, as Davies and a fellow student were walking down Maze Pond Street, they were attacked by men who tried to cut off their testicles.

Meanwhile Alderman Wood was steadily building up his case against George Edwards. Several people had made statements to him about the spy's activities, urging Wood to issue a warrant for his arrest. Reluctantly Wood refused, explaining that he was only a magistrate for the City, whereas the acts for which they wanted Edwards punished had been committed in Westminster and Middlesex. The proper course, he told them, was to apply to a magistrate for those places, or direct to Lord Sidmouth. Accepting this advice, his informants took written statements to the Home Office and left them there. Unfortunately they were valueless, because Wood was no more willing to swear the deponents than he was to issue a warrant.

In the House of Commons on 2 May Wood stated that some of the facts about Edwards were too horrible to repeat. In his opinion Edwards was an *agent provocateur* who had organised the Cato Street Conspiracy himself and then betrayed it for Blood Money, and he said that the Law Officers should be forced to explain why they had employed such a man. Also, since the Government knew where Edwards was hiding, it should produce him for questioning by the House.

The House was not greatly impressed, as most members could not believe that Edwards had instigated Thistlewood's plot. Mr. Hume expressed the view that Edwards, like many other spies, was not satisfied merely with giving information but had incited persons who were already guilty into committing further crimes. Nevertheless, he added, if Edwards really had suggested throwing grenades into Parliament, it was a serious matter; the plotting of such an act constituted 'a High Misdemeanour'.

Alderman Wood raised the subject of Edwards again on the ninth, mentioning some of the facts which had been too horrible to repeat on the second. He now claimed to have proof that Edwards was connected with a police officer who had been involved with Castle in the French prisoner scandal, and that Edwards had been seen near White Street at the time of Thistlewood's arrest.

Mr. Bankes said that in the depraved state of the present times, when men of such sanguinary dispositions were abroad, when such plots were embraced, not by one or two, but by a considerable number, was it not necessary for the Government to have recourse to spies? Had not Cicero received information from the courtesan Fulvia and the ambassadors of the Allobroges?

Mr. Denman said that in his opinion Castle was originally an accomplice, and it was well known that the Bank of England had spies who went down to the country with ready-made forged notes. (Cries of 'No!')

Mr. Canning remarked that because the worthy alderman had backed the Home Secretary's warrants in the City when he was Lord Mayor, he seemed to think that the Secretary of State was bound to return the compliment, by backing the alderman's bills of indictment from the other end of the town. Aldermen were great men! Lord Mayors were very great men! But the Secretary of State was not their servant.

The Attorney-General told the House that when Monument went before the Privy Council for examination he was handcuffed to Thistlewood, who told him to say that Edwards had seduced him into the plot. Monument asked him how he could say such a thing, when he had never even met Edwards? Thistlewood had replied that this did not matter, because he could describe to Monument what Edwards looked like and the sort of clothes he usually wore.

*   *   *

What of the man of mystery himself? On 25 February, two days after the fight in Cato Street, John Stafford had written Hobhouse a short letter in which he referred to Edwards as 'W——r'.

> When I left you I went directly to the Wheat Sheaf where I found W——r and conversed with him upon the subject you mentioned and appointed a place where he was to meet me soon afterwards. I went to the appointed Place, took a Room, had a Fire made, pens, paper, etc. provided and waited for him. I left and came to the office and returned, but he had not been, nor has he yet made his appearance.
>
> I have no doubt but he will call on you this Evening if I should not see him after dark. If he comes to you send him to the appointed place to-morrow morning. They will give me immediate notice of his presence.

Edwards dropped out of sight for over a month. Then in early May the Mayor of Cambridge wrote a strange letter to the Reverend Sir Henry Bate-Dudley, who was a well-known character in late Georgian London. A former editor of the *Morning Post*, whose readiness to fight a duel earned him the nickname of 'The Fighting Parson', he had written comic opera, served a term in the King's Bench Prison for libel, and often 'walked arm in arm with a fashionable beauty in the illuminated groves of

Vauxhall'.* In 1816, at the age of seventy, he had led a charge of
cavalry against rioting Fenland peasants.

The Mayor's letter informed Sir Henry that Edwards had
spent a week in Cambridge in April, under the 'pretence' of wanting to see an Italian who had been pirating his moulds. He had
been followed to the town by Palin.

> The postmaster still insists upon Edwards having been here
> this week [in May] but the Constables who have quietly
> endeavoured to trace him say he certainly has left the place.
> Palen or Peeling was certainly here but, owing to . . . a
> Gentleman who would not trust our Constables or me with
> the secret, escaped.
>
> I hope to be in Town previous to the Levee . . . I shall in-
> form you of the extraordinary conduct of Edwards whilst
> here – who must be a villain of the deepest dye – what he
> said I dare not trust in a letter. I think you will agree with
> me that I ought to lay the information before the proper
> persons at Lord Sidmouth's office.

Sir Henry sent this letter to Sidmouth with a covering note, in
which he said he was glad to hear that Edwards had 'shifted his
quarters' from Cambridge. He added that he had received
another private letter which confirmed that Edwards had stayed
in Cambridge for several days.

By this time, as it happened, Edwards had shifted his quarters
from England altogether. On 5 May he wrote to Hobhouse :

> According to your desire I gave all the papers I had in my
> possession together with the Copy of Depositions to the
> Gentlemen you sent to me on Sunday evening last – I am
> now in the Isle of Guernsey and think I may remain here in
> perfect safety till you direct otherwise.
>
> I beg leave to mention that my money will be exhausted
> by the time I can hear from you. I also beg leave to call

* Henry Angelo, op. cit.

your benevolent attention to my family whom I am sure
must want pecuniary assistance ere this reaches you. My
Goods, Moulds and Tools are locked up in my late lodgings
in Fleet Street were there is two Quarters rent due last Quarter day and as this Quarter is far advanced I dare say the
landlord will charge the three Quarters. Whatever way you
direct my wife to proceed in, she will get my brother to
accomplish . . . All letters I receive from you shall be Dis-
troyed as soon as Read.

Please Direct to me – G. E. Parker at Mr. Macey, New
Town, Isle of Guernsey.

Macey's was only a temporary billet for the Home Office spy,
who planned to emigrate as soon as his family could join him. On
8 May he wrote to Hobhouse again, asking him to procure a
passage for his mother-in-law as well. His wife, he explained, was
not looking forward to taking her four young children on a long
sea voyage to a strange land, but the thought of her mother going
with them would help to cheer her up.

As for myself, I am very bilious and labouring under a Con-
sumption . . . Should anything occur that induce you to
think it necessary that I pop over to France you will have
the goodness not to forget to send me a passport, and at the
same time to consult yourself about my safety in respect to
the name it be taken in, on account of the French Laws.

He also asked if he might enclose letters to his brother with his
Home Office correspondence, as he did not want to write to his
brother direct.

The reason is that I think it possible that a letter may per-
chance by the means of the Post Mark discover where I am,
knowing there has been a Radical employed for many years
in the Twopenny Post Office and possiblely may be some in
the General Post Office.

As he spoke of going to 'one of His Majesty's Colonies in the

East Indies', such caution seemed excessive; it seems likely that he was merely trying to cut down on postage by sending two letters in one envelope.

On 22 May a true bill for high treason was found against him by the Grand Jury for Middlesex. A man who was said to have made pikeheads for Thistlewood claimed that Edwards had ordered them and paid for them. Ironically, on this same date Edwards was writing to inform Hobhouse that he was thinking of returning to London, because two men who knew him by sight had arrived in the Channel Islands and might recognise him. 'It really seems I shall find it difficult to find a resting place,' he wrote. 'Perhaps London or its vicinity will be the safest.'

By the end of May he was writing to Hobhouse three times a week. On the twenty-eighth he said that there were a number of His Majesty's cutters, such as the *Starling*, plying between the Islands and Portsmouth. Since it was not safe for him to leave in a trading vessel, he wanted one of these cutters to pick him up and transfer him, with his family, to a ship bound for the Cape. Next day he wrote that his health was declining and obliged him to stay indoors for two or three days at a time.

At the end of the week he complained, 'I was charged Two Shillings and Fourpence for the last letter although it had been paid for double before it left England. The post man said it weighed one ounce.'

By 13 June he was very ill and in financial straits. 'I beg leave to mention that I have no money left except the last five pounds sent by Mr. Street and which I should be glad to be allowed to keep entire to carry me else were in case I should find it necessary to leave here.'

His wife and family were still in England. In the middle of June, John Stafford went to see Mrs. Edwards and reported to Hobhouse :

I have seen Mrs. E. Her husband has desired her to buy some things for him to take with her and says she must bring some money as he has very little. She intends to go on Tuesday morning. I have calculated the different sums she wants and find the whole amounts to £31 besides what he has had. Will you be good enough to say whether she may have it.

Hobhouse evidently sanctioned the payment. Edwards's family joined him on 7 July, and in a letter to Hobhouse he expressed his gratitude for 'the very handsome behaviour of Mr. Stafford'. By the twenty-fourth, however, he was out of funds and 'a trifle in debt', and said that he would be exceedingly obliged if some money could be sent by the next packet. 'I see by the *Times* newspaper,' he added, 'that Edwards the spy is in Dublin ! ! !'

Hobhouse sent off £20, for which Edwards wrote to thank him on 6 August saying that he had discovered that by taking a small house he could save himself about ten shillings a week. Unfortunately the broker who lent out furniture required a security of £70.

It was an odd state of affairs, if Alderman Wood's charges against Edwards were true. Here was a spy, only five months after he had betrayed a man who weighed a thousand pounds, trying to save himself half a sovereign a week.

For all his straitened circumstances Edwards was a lot better off than Robert Adams and Thomas Dwyer. Adams was in prison for debt and full of self-pity, while Dwyer was having great difficulty in getting work and in fear of his life. 'I am Fritefull of being assinated,' he wrote to Lord Sidmouth, 'by some of those Disafected people that serounds this Metropliss.' Another man who had suffered because of Thistlewood and his plot was the old teacher Thomas Hazard, who complained to the Home Office that no one would send their sons to his schoolroom any more and that his wife had lost her reason.

Hazard had been released in May, together with Preston, Simmons, Firth, George and Hall. Abel Hall, the tailor whom Adams had accused of helping to make the fireballs, had taken up where George Edwards left off. 'They all seem confident in me,' he informed the Home Office. 'There is no leader among them now.'

He said that Preston had done no work since his release, but spent most of his time drinking with anyone who would treat him. Firth and Robert George had seemingly given up politics and were devoting themselves to business: Firth had expanded and had bought two more cows. William Cooke was back in circulation and so was Potter, the shoemaker from Southwark. Palin was keeping very close, which was natural since he still weighed £200, but Potter had kept in touch with him, and even claimed to have seen him recently.

'I can get at him if wanted,' wrote Hall.

On 16 November Ruthven, Ellis and Westcott were given a special assignment by John Stafford. At about nine o'clock the following night, acting on information received, Ellis and Westcott went to Short's Gardens, Drury Lane, where they kept watch on a certain house. Presently several men emerged, one of them being a tall, shabbily-dressed man with a scowling look. Ellis, who was waiting at the street corner, let him go by; then rushed up behind him, pinioned his arms, and put a pistol to his head. Westcott stood in front of the man with a drawn cutlass, and offered to cut him down if he made the least resistance.

He was then taken to Bow Street, where Mr. Birnie took two short depositions about his identity, one from a man who had known the prisoner when he was in the East London Militia, and another from George Ruthven. Mr. Birnie then examined him.

MR. BIRNIE : What is your name?

PRISONER : John Palin.

MR. BIRNIE : I presume you know the nature of the charge upon which you are apprehended?

PRISONER : No, I do not; I am not at all aware of it.

MR. BIRNIE : Indeed! Well, Mr. Palin, you have given us a great deal of trouble, but here you are at last. It is my duty to inform you that you are charged with having been connected with Thistlewood, Tidd, and others, whom you well knew, in the conspiracies in which they were engaged, and which cost them their lives.

PRISONER : I deny the charge, and shall be able to rebut it.

MR. BIRNIE : Well, Sir, I hope you may.

A warrant of commitment was made out and Palin, heavily guarded, was taken to Coldbath Fields, where he remained a prisoner for the next six weeks. On 3 January 1821 he was questioned for over an hour by the Attorney-General and nine members of the Privy Council, to whom he swore that he had never meant to join Thistlewood in his 'horrid deed', but had tried to talk him out of doing it. He was bound over to keep the peace, in his own recognisance of £500, for seven years.

He thanked the Government for its leniency, and was discharged.

14
Questions and Clues

THISTLEWOOD believed that George Edwards turned to spying in 1819, but in this, as in so many other things, he was mistaken.

The names of the men who spied on Thistlewood, as we know, have been carefully erased from Home Office records, but a list of their occupations is obscurely filed in a box of papers relating to disturbances in the North of England. This list describes Hanley as a tradesman, Williamson as a weaver, Shegoe as an artisan. Early in 1818 there was a new recruit – 'a tradesman living out of London, recently introduced to the Secretary of State by a General Officer.'

This officer was Major-General Sir Herbert Taylor, the man who had patronised George Edwards's little model shop in Eton High Street. No one who aspired to be 'a Confidential Person' could have had a better sponsor, for Taylor had served as private secretary to King George III, Queen Charlotte, and the Duke of York.

From Windsor, Taylor wrote to Henry Hobhouse asking him to interview a man who was in distress. Largely through his brother, this man knew a good deal about Watson, Preston and company, and so long as he did not have to incriminate his brother he was willing to tell all he knew, and try to find out more. 'His name is W - - - r,' wrote Taylor, who signed himself 'A General Officer'.

On 27 January 1818, replying to 'Major General Taylor', Hobhouse wrote:

Sir,

I have to thank you for Your Letter of this Date, which I
have laid before Lord Sidmouth. Although we are aware of
great part of Transactions of the Persons named in Your
Letter, their Movements are of so much Consequence
that it would be wrong to reject any additional Testimony
on the Subject. I shall therefore be glad to have an Interview with Edwards; and as my private House is in a
quiet situation, not likely to be overlooked (Number 33
Grosvenor Place) I think that will be the most convenient
Place of Meeting. The Time must be either the Evening or
early in the Morning. If He will be in Town by Thursday
morning at 9 o'clock I will be ready to receive Him at that
Hour. You may assure Him that no use shall without his
consent be made of any Information given by Him, which
shall be prejudicial to Him; if such an Assurance should
be requisite to induce Him to see me.

So even before Thistlewood entered Horsham Gaol the man
whom he would make his ADC had offered to become a spy.

At his trial in 1820, Thistlewood referred to Edwards as 'the
contriver, the instigator, the entrapper . . . the suggestor and
promoter', but his counsel preferred to concentrate on Robert
Adams and his bizarre evidence, seeking to convince the jury
that Adams was lying. How could twenty-five paupers, asked
Adolphus, have hoped to capture the Bank of England and overthrow the Government?

Adams was not the first Crown witness, however, to accuse
Thistlewood of plotting to take the Tower and the Bank. Castle
had made the same charge in 1817. Admittedly he was not
the most convincing of witnesses: while Castle was giving
evidence, the Attorney-General had had to ask Watson's counsel
to stop holding up his hands in disbelief. Yet in the stories of
both Castle and Adams there were echoes of a trial which had
taken place long before Doctor Watson's, in a building on the
Surrey side of the river.

Thistlewood's main targets, Adams claimed, were the Tower,

the Bank, and the telegraphs; according to Thomas Windsor, they were also the primary targets of Colonel Despard. 'The mail coaches were to be stopped as a signal to the country,' said Windsor. 'We were to stop the Northern mails leaving London,' said Castle fourteen years later. 'Thistlewood will try to seize the Northern mail coaches,' Hobhouse warned Byng in 1819.

For the Crown, these repetitions were unfortunate. When prosecution witnesses told the same tales in one treason trial after another, it began to look as if State prisoners were being framed to a stale formula which the Law Officers or John Stafford were either too stupid or too arrogant to change. In retrospect it seems much more likely that even police spies and approvers sometimes told the truth, and that the Cato Street Conspiracy was based on the plan drawn up by Colonel Despard eighteen years before.

*　　　*　　　*

In accordance with Sir Herbert Taylor's will, most of his papers were destroyed shortly after his death in 1839 – a circumstance greatly regretted by Ernest Taylor, who arranged the remnant for publication in 1913. Had the general lived long enough to complete his memoirs, wrote Mr. Taylor, 'he would probably have left a very curious and fascinating narrative.'* He might also have shed some light on the man of mystery, George Edwards.

As it is, the significance of Edwards's visit to Cambridge, which so unsettled the Mayor and Sir Henry Bate-Dudley, has still to be discovered. Nor is it known how his brother William, said to have been a Bow Street policeman, was involved with Watson and company.[19] From August 1820 George Edwards alias G. E. Parker alias W - - - r vanishes from Home Office records, taking his secrets with him. At the time of his disappearance it was rumoured that he had sailed either to New Brunswick or the Cape of Good Hope.

Probably in the mid-1840s,* the Reverend Holt Okes conduc-

---

* *The Taylor Papers*, 1913.

† See F. R. Bradlow's article, 'A Sequel to the Cato Street Conspiracy', South African Library Quarterly Bulletin, vol. XXIII, no. 4, June 1969.

ted the burial of a man named Higgs, who had settled with his family at Wynberg near Cape Town. Okes, who had visited Higgs as he lay dying, believed him to have been banished to the Cape from England, where he had betrayed his associates in the plot known as the Cato Street Conspiracy. The reason for Okes's belief is not known, but it is assumed that Higgs made a death-bed confession to him. Unfortunately, Okes did not record Higgs's Christian name or the exact date of his death, but it is tempting to identify the man as John Williamson, who seems more likely to have made a deathbed confession than the other spies who settled at the Cape.[20]

On 13 June 1845, a John Higgs who may or may not have been Okes's communicant died at Plumstead, one mile south of Wynberg. Reporting this man's death, the *Cape Town Mail* for 21 June gave his birthplace as 'Chosley [sic], Berkshire', and the Cholsey Register of Births and Burials, which is preserved in the Berkshire Records Office at Reading, shows that he was born on 5 September 1779, the son of William and Sarah Higgs. Since his Christian name was John, and he was William's son, Higgs may well have taken the name John Williamson for his alias. If Williamson was right about his age being thirty-six in October 1817, he was two years younger than the John Higgs born at Cholsey, but some vagueness about their year of birth was not unusual among men of William's background.

Whoever the mysterious Higgs may have been, he was almost certainly not George Edwards; for in 1840, under 'Inhabitants of Cape Town and Environs', the *Cape Calendar and Annual Register* listed 'George Parker, modeller &c., green-point'. The possibility that this Parker was Edwards's son may be ruled out, because 'George Parker jun., lime burner &c., green-point' is listed in the same issue of the *Calendar*.

It seems safe to assume, therefore, that George Parker, modeller, of Green Point, and George Edwards, modeller, of Eton were one and the same man. When last heard of in Guernsey, Edwards was using the name of G. E. Parker, and in 1820, according to Aylmer, his age was about thirty-two. On 9 December 1843, the following announcement appeared in the

Deaths column of the *South African Commercial Advertiser* :

> Nov. 30. Mr. George Parker sen. aged 56 years.

Mr. Parker died owning property valued at £500 in Green Point, a district whose virtues were extolled in the *Cape of Good Hope Almanac* that year :

> Green Point is situated at the back of the Lion's Rump. On account of its proximity to Cape Town, combined with the pureness of the air and delightful refreshing breezes, it has become the resort of our merchants and men of business, who there find an agreeable retreat after the toil of the day.

15

Account Paid

———

London has changed greatly since Arthur Thistlewood's day. Coldbath Fields House of Correction has given way to the Mount Pleasant Sorting Office, the picaresque tenements of Wych Street to Bush House, Whitecross Street Prison to Barbican flats, and the Georgian slums of Fox Court to Victorian ones. But for anyone interested in the Cato Street Conspiracy there are still a few reminders to be tracked down or stumbled on. Hart Yard, on the west side of Brooke's Market, shows where the White Hart Tavern once stood, and a plaque in Chiswell Street marks the site of Caslon's vanished Type Foundry. A few yards away is Finsbury Street, once known as Artillery Court, which leads to what appears to be a cricket ground. Parked at the far end of it may be seen guns belonging to the Honourable Artillery Company.

Stone Buildings in Lincoln's Inn look much the same as they did when John Williamson reported there to Henry Litchfield, and the 'Spa Fields Gang' would have no difficulty in recognising Westminster Hall. Three Kings Court, where Doctor Watson once had his surgery, is now a backwater off Fleet Street, and hard to find unless one knows exactly where to look. The buildings which surround it are fairly modern, but at the head of a stair-well leading to a basement is a maculated wall which is clearly much older. Once there were sixteen cast-irons bars set vertically in its coping to form a paling, but only nine of them remain. The heads of these nine bars are all missing and appear to have been broken off, possibly by a sledge-hammer.

Running north off Lant Street, Southwark is a slit which suddenly turns east, south and west, ending in the cul-de-sac known as Vine Yard. The buildings are post-1820, but those maze-like twists of the narrow carriageway are eloquent of the sort of place in which men like John Palin used to live – places which it was easier to venture into than to leave, especially for anyone wearing a good watch on a foggy night in February.

There is no trace now of Isaac Bentley's smithy in Floral Street, Covent Garden; but his name is still preserved at the Public Record Office, in a box listed simply as T.S. 11/208-881 in the Treasury Solicitor's files. The box contains three rusty pikeheads, 'sharp at both ends, but one end jagged' – just as William Bayliss described them, except that they are almost twelve inches long. Tied to one of them is a small card on which is written, 'Specimen of pike similar to those made by I. Bentley, and to those alluded to in A.B.'s information.'

*   *   *

When Newgate Prison was demolished at the start of this century the bones buried in the passage known as The Graveyard presented quite a problem, as the burial site did not belong to the Prison Commissioners. They merely had a right of way over it, to enable them to take prisoners to the Old Bailey courts for trial, and it was said that the remains could only be exhumed and removed by Act of Parliament.

Fortunately, it transpired that the ground had never been consecrated; and as the flags of The Graveyard were part of a passage leading from one part of the gaol to another, the plot was not a burial ground within the meaning of the Disused Burial Grounds Act as amended by the Open Spaces Act. Over the years the bones beneath the flags had been dug up and re-buried many times, and whenever the ground was opened bones and skulls always came to light. They were carefully collected and replaced as near as possible to their original position. There was no way of identifying them, though it was known that the oldest remains dated from the year 1820.

The work began in November 1902, and by the following January seventy-three baskets had been filled with bones, including fifty-seven skulls. These were put into forty-six cases and re-interred in the City of London cemetery at Ilford, where a low iron rail was erected to mark the spot. Later in 1903, when a number of the prison's fittings and relics were auctioned, some of the people who attended the sale in Newgate were seen digging in the passage, apparently in search of the exhumed criminals' teeth. There was no report of anything being found.

However, according to a chart of the area which was available in 1902, ninety-seven people lay buried in the passage that year. The City of London's Medical Officer of Health thought that the oldest bones would have disappeared by that time, and indeed the bones which were later removed to Ilford represented the remains of ninety-two bodies. There were thus five sets of bones missing.

There is little doubt that Thistlewood and his friends were buried under the flags, because a photograph taken just before demolition shows the letters T B I D T carved in the wall of the passage : therefore it is possible that whatever remains of them is still there.*

'I shall soon be consigned to the grave,' Thistlewood had declared in 1820. 'My body will be immured beneath the soil whereon I first drew breath.'

Once again, and for the last time, events would prove him wrong.

* * *

Because of the notoriety which the conspiracy brought to Cato Street the residents succeeded in having it renamed Horace Street, but the name was changed back to Cato Street in 1937. On some Victorian maps, no name was given to the street at all.

Charles G. Harper, who wrote several books on London between the wars, was taken to see Horace Street as a boy, and found it very disappointing : it seemed to him that any locality where a plot to murder the Cabinet had been hatched ought to be more impressive to look at. When he went back in 1926 he found it just as squalid, a 'grey little purlieu' which had scarcely changed since his last visit.

---

* It is often assumed that all the bones of a corpse buried in quicklime are completely dissolved. A senior police officer, recently retired from the Metropolitan Police, assures me that this is not always so. D.J.

With this very important exception; the actual scene of the conspiracy and the fight has been swept away. It was at the John Street end and on the site now occupied by the double-doors which admit into the yard of the new and very large police station, rebuilt in 1905.*

Harper was searching for the stable on the wrong side of Cato Street; in fact, he was standing with his back to it. Even when the west side of the street was demolished in 1971 the little building survived, and is still instantly recognisable from drawings made in 1820. Inside, in place of the ladder used by Ruthven and his colleagues, a wooden staircase now leads up into the hayloft, in which most of the space is occupied by a large carpenter's bench.

One of the last survivors of the raid was John Shaw Strange,[21] the shoemaker transported to Australia for life, who became Chief Constable of the Bathurst district of New South Wales. Despite his lack of height Strange made an effective lawman, and obtained his ticket of leave for capturing a notorious bush-ranger single-handed. One of the constables who served under him was James Wilson, formerly of Fox Place, Marylebone; he eventually married again and went back to his old trade of tailoring.

Harrison also settled in Bathurst, where he opened a bakery. A judge who met him in 1830 described him as a muscular, forbidding-looking man, over six feet tall, with big dark eyes and thick, jet-black hair. The judge thought him rather simple-minded, especially when he boasted that Thistlewood had promised to make him Lord Chancellor.†

Richard Birnie died in 1832, having achieved his great ambition. In 1821, when a riot seemed imminent at Queen Caroline's funeral, Sir Robert Baker‡ failed to take control, and Birnie read the Riot Act on his own initiative. When Baker re-

---

* Charles G. Harper, *A Londoner's Own London*, 1927.
    † R. Therry, *Reminiscences of Thirty Years' Residence in New South Wales and Victoria*, 1863.
    ‡ Knighted 10 May 1820.

signed as Chief Magistrate soon afterwards, Birnie got the post
that he had coveted so long and the knighthood that went with
it. One of his first tasks was to deal with a complaint that
members of the Bow Street Patrol were calling at the Hanoverian
Consul's house to solicit Christmas boxes.

Sir Richard's bad temper and arrogance continued to make
him enemies. Fitzgerald tells us that, arriving late at a meeting of
the Covent Garden Overseers, Birnie found that in his absence
a certain Mr. Dow had volunteered to act as Chairman. When
Birnie brusquely asked for an explanation, Dow introduced
himself, saying that he was ready to resign the chair.

'Get out, sir! Get out!' Birnie shouted, and seized the man
by his arm, which was dislocated and held in a sling.

'Gently, Sir Richard!' Dow pleaded. 'You do not consider
my arm, you give me great pain.'

'I care nothing for your arm!' the Chief Magistrate replied.*

Sir Richard naturally resented the decline in Bow Street's
power and influence which marked his last years in office. In
1829 the Patrols were absorbed into Peel's New Police, but the
Bow Street Runners were allowed to have a separate existence
for ten years more. Sir John Moylan, an implacable critic of the
old system, claims that they kept all the lucrative robbery cases
for themselves and left murders for the Peelers to solve.† According to a memorandum entitled *Hints for Improving the New
Police,* which was sent to Scotland Yard in 1832, the Peelers
were constantly being obstructed by officials of the bad old
system: 'jealous magistrates, prejudicial clerks and corrupt
officers, from Sir Richard Birnie downwards,' – men who had
enjoyed too much 'familiarity' with their masters at the Home
Office. 'This familiarity extended from the Magistrates to the
officers and to "Stafford's men", as they were called – persons
who, acting as *spies,* made themselves important by giving
imaginary importance to the contemptible ravings or wild
theories of political quacks in the humbler grades of society.'

The author of this document was Vincent George Dowling,

* Percy H. Fitzgerald, op. cit.
† J. F. Moylan, *Scotland Yard and the Metropolitan Police,* Putnam, 1934

the man whom Stafford had sent to eavesdrop on Doctor Watson in Whitecross Street Prison.

When the Runners were finally disbanded in 1839, George Ruthven retired with thirty years' service. He became landlord of the One Tun and King's Arms in Chandos Street, Covent Garden, and died in 1844 at the early age of fifty-two. 'He was a most eccentric character,' said the *Times* obituary, 'and had written a history of his life, but would on no account allow it to meet the public eye.'

*   *   *

In September 1837, at the age of seventy-one, John Stafford died at his home on Scots Hill, Rickmansworth. He left all his wordly goods to his dear wife Sarah, including the flag taken at Spa Fields in 1816, which was one of his most valued possessions.

When Peel was Home Secretary, according to the *Times* obituary, Stafford was offered the post of police magistrate, but he turned it down – 'from a feeling, perhaps, of diffidence in his own abilities, and a natural desire not to obtrude himself into a situation which would necessarily bring him so frequently before the public.' The paper continued :

> His sound knowledge of criminal law, his consummate skill in the framing of indictments, and his long practical acquaintance with the duties which devolved upon him, caused him very frequently to be consulted by the ablest criminal lawyers of the day.
>
> When the Cato Street Conspiracy was fully detected and the capture of the party determined upon, Mr. Stafford volunteered his services to head the Bow Street officers who distinguished themselves on that occasion, although his duties as Chief Clerk by no means required that he should hazard his person in such a desperate enterprise. He had prepared his pistols and made the necessary arrangements when, just as he was about to join the officers and proceed to the scene of action, a message from the Home Office requiring his immediate attendance compelled him to

forego his intention. He gave his pistols to the brave but ill-fated Smithers.

It seems very strange that Stafford, with his brilliant operational record and his interest in the case, should not have been in at the death. The urgent business which called him to the Home Office that night remains a mystery. Whatever it was, it probably saved his life; for if Stafford had led the raid on Cato Street, Thistlewood would certainly have tried to kill him.

Smithers, with his fatal likeness to the man whose pistols he carried, died in Stafford's place – a tragic event which was not without its advantages. Thistlewood, after all, had got away with high treason once before; but with the killing of Smithers his luck ran out. All that remained to be decided, as Adolphus remarked at Thistlewood's trial, was whether or not his corpse should be dissected.

*   *   *

To modern eyes, Thistlewood and his gimcrack army of Spenceans and Old Jacks may seem ludicrous, but viewed against the squalor and brutality of Regency London they appeared in rather a different light. A fanatic bent on turning the city into a shambles, with slum-dwellers bearing aristocrats' heads along Oxford Street and a Committee of Public Safety sitting at the Mansion House, was not a joke to anyone who had met fugitives from the Terror. It is not surprising that the men who risked their lives to put him 'out of the world' were well rewarded.

In 1881 Bow Street Public Office moved to new premises on the opposite side of the street, and the old buildings were eventually demolished. The records were mostly destroyed, since they were deemed to be of no further use or interest. Fortunately the Office accounts for 1820 and a few other years are preserved at the Public Record Office, and details of certain other payments made by the Chief Magistrate can be traced through Home Office and Treasury correspondence.

Smithers's widow was granted a pension of £100, and at the King's suggestion a pension of £30 was awarded to his parents.

For assisting the civil power at Cato Street the Coldstream Guards were alloted the sum of eighty-five guineas : each private of the picquet guard was paid two guineas, while their corporal received five guineas and the two sergeants ten guineas each.

The police officers who took part in the raid received a total of £333, of which Ruthven and Ellis received almost half; because of their exemplary conduct they were paid £100 and £50 respectively. The £200 reward for John Palin was not paid until the following year; in the meantime, for his services during the trials of the Cato Street conspirators, Mr. John Stafford was awarded the sum of £150.

On 19 July 1820 a petition to Lord Sidmouth was drawn up by Stephen Lavender, Daniel Bishop and William Salmon, Constables belonging to the Bow Street Public Office. This petition recalled that on 24 February, on orders from R. Birnie Esquire, his lordship's memorialists had proceeded with several of the Patrol to White Street, Finsbury, where they did at great hazard take and apprehend one Arthur Thistlewood. His lordship's memorialists therefore humbly conceived that they and the Patrol were entitled to the reward of One Thousand Pounds. On this document the Home Office noted : 'N.B. Ruthven was also present. Write to Treasury for payment of the Reward to Mr. R. Baker (as was done in 1817).'[22]

*   *   *

In 1822, giving evidence to a Select Committee studying London's police system, Sir Richard Birnie was asked if police officers had any allowance when they were wounded; and whether, in the event of their losing their lives in the service, there was any pension for their families.

'I believe not,' he replied. 'There was a man of the name of Smithers lost his life about two years ago in Cato Street; a very handsome provision was made by Government, and a large subscription raised. But that was a peculiar case.'

Notes on the Text

[1] Seven more Public Offices were created by Act of Parliament in 1792, at Queen Square, Great Marlborough Street, Hatton Garden, Worship Street, Whitechapel, Shadwell and Union Hall, Southwark. The Thames Police Office at Wapping was set up in 1798.

[2] In 1793, aged twenty-two, Place led a strike of London breeches-makers, and found it so difficult to get work afterwards that he nearly starved. In 1799 he opened a tailoring business in Charing Cross Road. A tireless researcher and organiser, he made a tremendous contribution to the cause of Radical reform, notably by providing orators and journalists with material for their speeches and writings.

[3] All Doctor Watson's bolt-holes had been searched after his capture the previous December. Nonetheless, on 5 March a Bow Street Officer went to the house in Hyde Street and found 199 pikeheads in the privy. He cleaned them up as best he could and carried them away in a box.

[4] Wetherell, who defended Watson so skilfully, was a lifelong Tory, but his hopes of being appointed Attorney-General had recently been disappointed. He was furious with the Establishment.

[5] The Attorney-General was not entirely ignorant of Castle's record. On 30 July 1812, reporting the Guildford forgery trial, *The Times* noted: 'Mr. Serjeant Shepherd stated the case to the jury: a man of the name of John Castle (who was in custody at Clerkenwell Prison) was fixed upon for the purpose of detecting Davis, he having previously bought forged notes of him . . . Castle was supplied by Mr. Westwood, Clerk to Messrs. Winter and Kaye, the Solicitors to the Bank, with good notes to purchase forged ones of the prisoner.'

[6] Despard and his men were sentenced to be hanged, drawn and quartered – i.e. disembowelled alive. The quartering was remitted. They were 'drawn' round the prison yard on a wooden hurdle pulled by a draught horse, then taken to the gallows and hanged by the neck until dead.

[7] The details of Castle's recruitment as a spy will be found in H.O. 42/160.

[8] Henry Hobhouse was Keeper of State Papers from 1826 until his death in 1854 – the year in which this report of Hanley's was found.

[9] There was a rumour current at this time that the Regent had bribed Sir Richard Croft, who attended the pregnant Princess, to kill both her and her baby. It gained ground (especially in Lincolnshire) when Croft shot himself. A lawyer at Louth wrote to the Home Office saying that it was probably invented by either Thistlewood's or two of Watson's brothers, all of whom lived in the neighbourhood of Louth.

[10] In 1818 the London garrisons included:

The Life Guards (Hyde Park and King Street)	848 men
1st Foot Guards (The Tower)	937 men
2nd Foot Guards (Portman Barracks)	773 men
3rd Foot Guards (Knightsbridge and Westminster)	1597 men

[11] Three months earlier the Treasury had written to Henry Hobhouse: 'Re your letter transmitting one from John Castle complaining of a charge made against him for using a two-wheel carriage, this is liable to duty as a two-wheel carriage and consequently the horse is liable to duty.' (T. 28/48 f. 214.) This suggests that Castle had retired to Yorkshire with his 'pair of plates' – the hackney carriage licence which it was supposed to be every police informer's ambition to earn.

[12] Williamson had been a spy for well over two years, and no doubt the Treasury Solicitor felt that he had earned his retirement. Several Home Office spies went to the Cape of Good Hope after they had been allowed to resign.

[13] One of Watson's visitors was an East India Company employee, who talked about politics and Company affairs, mentioning that whereas the Company would once have been able to raise three dependable battalions, there were not now enough good men to raise more than one. The Company's Chairman was told of this conversation a few days later by a letter from Henry Hobhouse.

[14] Charles Knight, who visited Edwards at his shop, described him as 'a diminutive animal with downcast look and stealthy face' (*Passages of a Working Life*, 1864). According to a description published in *The Times*, Edwards was only five feet three inches tall.

[15] Soon afterwards Waddington retired from printing and publishing to become a tallow chandler's porter.

[16] The officers who went to Tidd's on 24 February did much better, bringing away eleven bags of gunpowder, 965 ball cartridge and ten grenades. According to Tidd, when Ruthven searched him at Cato Street he exclaimed in disgust, 'Curse me, there's nothing here but a tobacco box.'

¹⁷ The hangman was James Botting, a morose character who was said to have the mentality of a slaughterman. He rarely spoke to 'the party', as he called a condemned man or woman.

¹⁸ An axe which had been specially made for the decapitation was not used. It is now in the London Museum.

¹⁹ Edwards certainly had a brother who was a policeman. In one of his reports he wrote: 'The City Police can not be depended on, many of them are favourable to the disaffected. This I know from my brother.'

²⁰ Oliver the spy retired to the Cape under his real name of W. O. Jones, and was appointed Inspector of Public Buildings and Chimneys. He died at Wynberg in 1827.

²¹ John Shaw Strange was still alive in 1869. According to Philip Benton, the Essex antiquary, an old shoemaker named Johnson, who was living in Rochford in 1872, claimed to have been a member of Brunt's London circle in his youth. He never attended any of the meetings. He was actually on his way to the stable in Cato Street on 23 February, but when he reached a public house called The Good Woman, something made him turn back. (See Philip Benton, *The History of Rochford Hundred,* vol. 1.)

²² The phrase 'as was done in 1817' suggests that the £500 reward for Thistlewood's arrest in 1817 was also paid to Baker: in fact it was paid to his predecessor as Chief Magistrate, Sir Nathaniel Conant, who distributed it to the officers concerned. The payment is recorded in the Treasury Solicitor's Accounts Ledger for 1818 (A.O. 3, 1104, 12 January 1818). The Treasury Solicitor's account books, which are filed under the Audit Office class of Treasury papers at the Public Record Office, contain much fascinating information, such as the costs incurred in sending Oliver to Derby, and in securing a pardon for George Edwards.

Sources

The primary material for Thistlewood and his plots is contained in approximately 100 boxes of unbound manuscripts at the Public Record Office. Some boxes, such as those listed under Class T.S.11, are devoted exclusively to Thistlewood and his associates; the words 'Thistlewood Papers' are pencilled on the back of many of these documents. Other boxes contain Thistlewood Papers filed chronologically with a mass of MSS. which have no bearing on Thistlewood at all: boxes in Class H.O. 42, for example, contain miscellaneous Home Office correspondence dealing with a wide range of subjects, the only common denominator being the date of origin.

The following list of Piece Numbers, arranged by chapters, identifies those boxes of MSS. at the Public Record Office which (a) have been freely used to research the chapter, or (b) contain relevant documents of particular interest. Most of these Piece Numbers refer to boxes of loose MSS. A few represent bound ledgers containing either hand-written copies of Out Letters (as in the case of T. 28/48), or shorthand writers' transcripts, chiefly of the trials.

Public Record Office Class References are abbreviated as follows:

H.O.	Home Office	K.B.	King's Bench
MEPOL	Metropolitan Police	P.C.	Privy Council
T.	Treasury	T.S.	Treasury Solicitor
W.O.	War Office		

CHAPTER I

H.O. 40/3(3)	H.O. 42/157	T.S. 11/199-868
H.O. 40/7(10)	H.O. 42/160	T.S. 11/200-869
H.O. 40/10(2)	H.O. 42/161	T.S. 11/201-870
H.O. 41/25	H.O. 42/181	T.S. 11/202-872
H.O. 42/153	H.O. 44/4	T.S. 11/203-873
H.O. 42/155	T.S. 11/198-863	T.S. 11/204-875
H.O. 42/156	T.S. 11/198-865	T.S. 11/1031-4431

CHAPTER 2

H.O. 40/3(3)	H.O. 42/158	H.O. 79/10
H.O. 40/3(4)	H.O. 42/159	T.S. 11/203-873
H.O. 40/10(2)	H.O. 42/160	T.S. 11/203-874
H.O. 42/156	H.O. 42/168	T.S. 11/204-875

CHAPTER 3

H.O. 42/165	H.O. 79/3	T.S. 11/199-867
H.O. 42/166	K.B. 33-9/2	T.S. 11/199-868
H.O. 42/167	T.S. 11/131-351	T.S. 11/202-871
H.O. 44/4	T.S. 11/198-863	T.S. 11/203-873

CHAPTER 4

H.O. 40/7(10)	K.B. 8/87	T.S. 11/199-867
H.O. 42/164	T.S. 11/121-332	T.S. 11/204-875
H.O. 42/169	T.S. 11/121-333	T.S. 11/906-3099

CHAPTER 5

H.O. 40/7(1)	H.O. 40/9(4)	H.O. 42/179
H.O. 40/7(2)	H.O. 41/25	H.O. 79/3
H.O. 40/8(1)	H.O. 42/169	T.S. 11/197-859
H.O. 40/8(2)	H.O. 42/170	T.S. 11/203-873
H.O. 40/8(3)	H.O. 42/171	

CHAPTER 6

H.O. 40/7(4)	H.O. 42/179	K.B. 33-9/3
H.O. 40/8(3)	H.O. 42/180	T. 28/48
H.O. 40/8(4)	H.O. 42/181	T.S. 11/134-359
H.O. 40/9(5)	H.O. 42/182	T.S. 11/197-859
H.O. 42/158	H.O. 42/186	T.S. 11/198-866
H.O. 42/171	H.O. 42/187	T.S. 11/201-870
H.O. 42/173	H.O. 42/189	T.S. 11/204-875
H.O. 42/174	H.O. 42/190	
H.O. 42/177	H.O. 42/192	

CHAPTER 7

H.O. 42/190	H.O. 42/195	H.O. 79/4
H.O. 42/191	H.O. 42/197	T.S. 11/197-859
H.O. 42/193	H.O. 42/198	T.S. 11/204-875
H.O. 42/194	H.O. 42/201	

CHAPTER 8

H.O. 40/8(3)	H.O. 42/199	T.S. 11/199-867
H.O. 42/196	H.O. 44/5	T.S. 11/203-874
H.O. 42/197	H.O. 79/4	T.S. 11/205-876

CHAPTER 9

H.O. 42/199	T.S. 11/199-867	T.S. 11/203-874
H.O. 44/4	T.S. 11/201-870	T.S. 11/204-875
H.O. 44/5	T.S. 11/202-871	T.S. 11/205-876

CHAPTER 10

H.O. 42/167	P.C. 1/4192	T.S. 11/205-876
H.O. 44/5	T.S. 11/199-867	T.S. 11/205-877

CHAPTER 11

H.O. 42/167	H.O. 79/4	P.C. 1/4192
H.O. 42/171	T.S. 11/199-868	W.O. 94/60(4)
H.O. 44/5	T.S. 11/204-875	

CHAPTER 12

H.O. 40/13	H.O. 79/4	T.S. 11/205-876
H.O. 41/26	T.S. 11/201-870	T.S. 11/206-879
H.O. 44/5	T.S. 11/204-875	T.S. 11/207-880
H.O. 44/6		

CHAPTER 13

H.O. 41/6	H.O. 44/6	T.S. 11/204-875
H.O. 41/26		

CHAPTER 14

H.O. 40/8(4)	H.O. 79/3	T.S. 11/906-3099
H.O. 40/9(4)	T.S. 11/121-332	

CHAPTER 15

H.O. 41/6	H.O. 45/9993/A46562	T. 28/49
H.O. 41/26	H.O. 45/9994/A46562	T. 38/674
H.O. 44/6	MEPOL 2/5799	T.S. 11/208-881

STATE PAPERS

Report from the Committee of Secrecy (*Reports, Committees,* 1817, *iv*).
Second Report of the Committee of Secrecy (*Reports, Committees,* 1817, *iv*).
Report of the Secret Committee of the House of Lords (*Reports, Committees,* 1817, *iv*).
Report from the Committee on the State of the Police of the Metropolis, 1816 (*Reports, Committees,* 1816, *v*).
First Report from the Committee on the State of the Police of the Metropolis, 1817 (*Reports, Committees,* 1817, *vii*).

Report from the Select Committee on the Police of the Metropolis, 1822
(*Reports, Committees*, 1822, *iv*).
Report from the Select Committee on Metropolis Police Officers, 1837
(*Reports, Committees*, 1837, *xii*).

CONTEMPORARY PUBLICATIONS

Anti-Gallican
Annual Register
Bell's Weekly Messenger
Black Dwarf
The Briton
The Cap of Liberty
Cobbett's Evening Post
Courier
Cowdroy's Manchester Gazette
The Day
Edmonds's Weekly Recorder
The Gentleman's Magazine
Hansard's Parliamentary Debates
Hone's Reformists' Register
The Hue & Cry and Police Gazette
Independent Whig
The Ledger
Leeds Mercury
The London Alfred, or People's
    Recorder

London Chronicle
London Gazette
Manchester Mercury
Manchester Observer
The Medusa, or Penny Politician
Morning Chronicle
Morning Herald
New Times
Nottingham Review and General
    Advertiser
Observer
Old Bailey Sessions
The Republican
Sherwin's Political Register
The Star
The Theological & Political Comet,
    or Free-thinking Englishman
The Times
The Traveller

Bibliography

Allen, Thomas, *The History and Antiquities of the Parish of Lambeth*, 1820.

Angelo, Henry, *The Reminiscences of Henry Angelo*, 1830.

Armitage, Gilbert, *The History of the Bow Street Runners* 1729-1829, Wishart & Co., 1932.

Aylmer, Edward, *The Memoirs of George Edwards*, 1820.

Bamford, Samuel, *Passages in the Life of a Radical*, 1841-43.

Berguer, Lionel Thomas, *A Warning Letter to H.R.H. the Prince Regent*, 1819.

Berguer, Lionel Thomas, *A Second Warning Letter to H.R.H. the Prince Regent*, 1819.

Cobbett, William, *Cobbett's Complete Collection of State Trials*, vols. 28, 32 & 33, 1809-26.

Darvall, Frank Ongley, *Popular Disturbances and Public Order in Regency England*, Oxford University Press, 1969.

Finch, W., *Religion! Liberty! and Laws!!! Reflections on the Case of Despard and His Unfortunate Associates*, 1803.

Fitzgerald, Percy H., *Chronicles of Bow Street Police Office*, 1888.

Fearon, Henry Bradshaw, *Sketches of America*, 1818.

Fyvie, John, *Noble Dames and Notable Men of the Georgian Era*, 1910.

Hackwood, Frederick W., *William Hone, His Life and Times*, 1912.

Harper, Charles G., *A Londoner's Own London*, Palmer, 1927.

Henderson, Emily, *Recollections of the Public Career and Private Life of the Late John Adolphus*, 1871.

Hone, William, *Bartholomew Fair Insurrection and the Pie-Bald Poney Plot*, 1817.

Hone, William, *The Meetings at Spa Fields*, 1816.

Hone, William, *The Riots in London*, 1816.

Hyde, H. Montgomery, *The Strange Death of Lord Castlereagh*, Heinemann, 1959.

Knight, Charles, *Passages of a Working Life*, 1864.

Moylan, J. F., *Scotland Yard and the Metropolitan Police*, Putnam, 1934.

Neal, J., *The Pentrich Revolution*, 1895.

Oman, C. W. C., *The Unfortunate Colonel Despard and Other Studies*, 1922.

Patterson, M. W., *Sir Francis Burdett and His Times*, Macmillan, 1931.

Preston, Thomas, *The Life and Opinions of Thomas Preston, Patriot and Shoemaker*, 1817.

Richmond, Alex B., *Narrative of the Condition of the Manufacturing Population*, 1825.

Robinson, Henry Crabb, *Diary, Reminiscences and Correspondence of Henry Crabb Robinson*, 1869.

Romilly, Sir Samuel, *Memoirs of the Life of Sir Samuel Romilly*, 1840.

Shelley, P. B., *We Pity the Plumage but Forget the Dying Bird, by 'The Hermit of Marlowe,'* 1817.

Shepherd, Henry John, *Memoir of the Right Honourable Samuel Shepherd*, 1841.

Stanhope, John, *The Cato Street Conspiracy*, Jonathan Cape, 1962.

Taylor, Ernest, *The Taylor Papers*, 1913.

Therry, R., *Reminiscences of Thirty Years' Residence in New South Wales and Victoria*, 1863.

Twiss, Horace, *The Public and Private Life of Lord Chancellor Eldon*, 1844.

Wade, J., *A Treatise on the Police and Crimes of the Metropolis*, 1829.

Wilkinson, George Theodore, *An Authentic History of the Cato Street Conspiracy*, 1820.

Wilkinson, George Theodore, *The Newgate Calendar Improved*, 1820.

Ziegler, Philip, *Addington*, Collins, 1965.

The Blackfaces of 1812, 1839.

Fairburn's Edition of the Whole Proceedings of the Trial of James Watson Senior, 1817.

Memoirs of the Life of Colonel E. M. Despard with His Trial at Large, 1803.

Memoirs of the Life of Colonel M. Despard, 1803.

Spies and Bloodites!! The Lives and Political History of Those Arch-Fiends Oliver, Reynolds & Co., 1817.

The Trials at Large of Arthur Thistlewood, James Watson, Thomas Preston and John Hooper, 1817.

The Trials of Arthur Thistlewood, James Ings, J. T. Brunt, Richard Tidd, William Davidson and Others for High Treason, 1820.

The Whole Four Trials of the Thief Takers, 1816.

The Whole Proceedings of the Trials of Colonel Despard and the other State Prisoners, 1803.

Index of Persons Mentioned in the Text

Inclusive numbers signify consecutive pages on which references occur rather than extended coverage of the subject.